FROM STREET GANG
CLUBS TO SOCIAL WORKER

THE
RIDE
OF MY
LIFE

A MEMOIR
JUSTIN "MOOCH" DELORETTO

Cover photo credit: Mike Dash/Kings Media

Printed in the United States of America

Hardcover ISBN: 978-1-961624-17-7
Paperback ISBN: 978-1-961624-18-4
Ebook ISBN: 978-1-961624-19-1
Library of Congress Control Number: 2023945090

DartFrog Blue
A division of DartFrog Books
https://dartfrogbooks.com

ACKNOWLEDGMENTS

IT HAS OFTEN BEEN said that you can judge a man by the company he keeps. I have been very grateful in this life to have been surrounded by some of the best family and friends a man could ever ask for. Without them, this book would not have been possible, and I wanted to take a moment to thank some of them. Everyone I have met on this journey has played a role, and there is not enough time or space here to thank them all. Those who subscribe to and watch my YouTube channel, those who follow me and interact with me on social media, and anyone who has every supported me or offered a kind word, I appreciate you all, thank you.

Bryan Denson, who used to be a journalist for the *Oregonian* newspaper. Bryan covered pretty much any story that had to do with me since starting the Mongols in Oregon in 2007, to my arrest and subsequent criminal trial, to my verdict, all of the times I violated probation, left the state, and the big Black Rain Raids of 2008. Bryan even wrote a story about my lawsuit against the Oregon Youth Authority during my final year of graduate school. I spoke to Bryan when I was thinking about writing a book, and he gave me some great advice as well as the motivation to do it. Bryan helped me realize that my story is important to tell, and that people will want to hear it.

My good friend, jiu jitsu professor, Tom DeBlass. Tom also has a memoir out (read it if you haven't yet), and when I was picking his brain about the process, he hooked me up with the crew at DartFrog

Books. Without that introduction, I don't know if this book would have happened. Thank you so much, Tom, and the incredible team at DartFrog.

To my mother, who has always done anything she could for us. I would not be where I am today without her blind loyalty and unconditional love. We didn't make it easier for her, but she always acted like we did. Thank you, Mom, I love you.

To my entire family, for always being in my corner, supporting me, loving me, and keeping us all well fed.

To my stepfather, who taught me the value of hard work, and the importance of being a man of your word.

To my father, he may not have been there a lot in my early years, but he has gone above and beyond to make up for it in my adult years, and I appreciate him very much.

To my twin brother, who always remembers things differently than me and probably will get frustrated early on in this book and not finish it. From birth to now, we have done everything together, for the most part, so a lot of these stories are his as well.

To Fishnets and all of the members of The Escaped. We toured the country in our early twenties with no cell phones or navigation, and proved that you can do whatever you set your mind to, and that there is no substitute for hard work. To anyone who ever gave us a place to stay, came to our shows, helped book our tours, or put out our records, you made those years very memorable.

To the Rose City Bovver Boys, past and present. The older generation taught me a lot about leadership and the importance of being a man of your word. A lot of what I took with me into the motorcycle club world I learned from my time with RCBB. I am honored to still have many of you in my life as close friends and mentors.

To the members of the Mongols Motorcycle Club, who I spent countless hours on the road with, late nights in hotel rooms, and traveled all over the world with. Thank you for the brotherhood and great times.

To Heath Pedigo and all of my teammates at Pedigo Submission Fighting for giving me the brotherhood and family I needed in a time I needed it the most.

To everyone who believes in and supports the Lift Train Ride Movement and chooses to strive to better themselves and those around them. And to the members of LTR who showed anyone who was watching what the true meaning of loyalty and honor really are.

To Frank and Tammy Curley. After they lost their son, my club brother, Blane, we have become family, and in his honor, I will do anything I can for you both, always.

To my own brother, Kyle, who died at the age of eleven before we got to experience a lot of life together. I know how happy he would have been about this book as he was my biggest fan.

To all of the professors and faculty at Whittier College and George Fox University who treated me as an equal even when I was twenty years older than most of the other students. They believed in me and supported me when it mattered. Thank you.

And last by not least, to my beautiful and amazing wife, Ashley. For she has loved me unconditionally, through thick and thin. She has been the light in my darkest days. My adventure partner, my best friend, confidant, and biggest supporter. I would not be the man I am today without her.

IN MEMORY OF...

I DEDICATE THIS BOOK TO those who have died before me. Everyone honored below played a role in my life and I am grateful to have known them and spent time with them when I had the chance.

My grandmother, Virginia DeLoretto

My grandfather, Louis DeLoretto

My brother, Kyle Rabe

Ryan Young

Smiley B (RCBB/Free Souls MC)

Tane (RCBB)

Big Dan (Outsiders MC)

Springer (Outsiders MC)

Matlock (Outsiders MC)

Joker Jason (Gypsy Jokers MC)

Wild Bill (Vagos MC)

Slider (Vagos MC)

Rambler (Mongols MC)

Dirty Ernie (Mongols MC)

Needles (Mongols MC)

Lil Peeka (Mongols MC)

Ox (Mongols MC)

Tulsa Jeff (Mongols MC)

Cholo (Mongols MC)

Chacho (Mongols MC)

Beast (Mongols MC)

Knuckles (Mongols MC)

Chamaco (Mongols MC)

The Rev (Mongols MC)

Short Stack (Mongols MC)

Big Balls (Mongols MC)

Lenny (Mongols MC)

TNT (Mongols MC)

Blane "Scoops" Curley (Mongols MC)

Tug (Pagans MC)

Rage (Pagans MC)

Orlando Sanchez

Rhino (Carson Skins)

CHAPTER ONE

THERE ARE THINGS THAT everyone knows. I have lived long enough to know that, when everyone knows something, the something everyone knows is probably wrong. In fact, I'm a walking example of the fact. You see a guy, a young guy, he's a biker, he's in a club, he's always in fights, the police take an interest, he does some jail time–not a lot, but then he does some more–so you know his background. Broken family. No ambition. Neglected. Beaten as a child. Well, I was that young guy, I was a biker (still am), I was in a club, and if you didn't see me fighting, I was probably asleep at the time. That was me. But the rest of it? Doesn't describe me at all. Italian families come in all shapes and sizes, but what every one of them has in common is Love. Capital *L*. They are hugging, loving, embracing families who care about all their members and look after them. And mine fit that description. Totally.

I was born in Salem, Oregon in 1981. I should really say "we were born" because I have a twin brother, Jeremy. Here, if you like, you could stretch the evidence as far as it will go because my biological father had been in and out of the care system growing up, he'd been a troublemaker in high school, and he wasn't around much after my brother and I arrived, not least because he was often in prison. In 1990, for example, when I was nine, he was sentenced to ninety-seven months in federal prison for conspiracy to distribute cocaine. But you would be stretching because as my father is not how I see him. I know him, we're in touch, I see him as a friend.

Someone it's cool to meet up with, have a beer with, shoot the breeze with, but if it came right down to it, not someone I'd want to rely on. And I don't need to because when we were still in grade school our mother married someone else, giving us a stepfather. He was much more reliable–a good man in every respect–but he worked very hard for long hours, and when he wasn't at the work he was employed to do, he'd be working on projects at home and on the farm he owned, so we didn't spend a lot of time together. He did all the fatherly things–came to every school meeting and every sporting event we were involved in, took us on vacations, and loved being a father. But the man who was really a father figure to me when I was growing up was my grandfather. He taught me about compassion, how to treat a woman, pretty much everything I know. If I wanted to talk things over, he was the one I went to. He and my grandma also came to all of our wrestling matches and sporting events. My grandparents were a huge part of my life until Grandpa died in 2001.

Mom had four children altogether; as well as Jeremy and me, she had two with my stepfather. My half-brother Kyle was born in 1991 and died at the age of eleven in an ATV accident while riding on the neighbor's farm. That hit our family really hard, but a few years later, they decided to have another child and my half-sister Kyleah was born.

Mom and my biological father had been dating since high school, and she had that failing common to young women drawn to 'bad guys'–the idea that she could change him. Becoming pregnant probably kept them together a little longer than they might have been otherwise, but they never married. Mom was twenty-two when my brother and I were born, and she moved back with her parents, my grandparents, when she found out she was pregnant. They were both schoolteachers and sports coaches, and in the early days, they had most of the raising of me and my brother, so we didn't lack intelligent, loving care and guidance.

I mentioned the Italian influence. My grandparents had been raised in New Jersey and moved out to Oregon to go to college and get their teaching degrees. Their parents had come to America from Italy. Italian families tend to be very tight-knit. Every week was a family dinner, we regularly got together in extended family formation for weddings and celebrations or just because we felt like it, and hugs and kisses were something you became used to. You considered them your right.

My stepfather was a mechanical engineer with several masters degrees and a good job, and when I was in grade school, we lived in a middle class area, but he had property outside the city, and we moved there so I enrolled in junior high in a small country area. That was probably where my early trouble started. We were city kids and identical twins so we stood out in two ways. In a country school like that, there's never any shortage of young guys full of testosterone who know what jobs they're going to be doing as adults and see no point in getting an education. What they do see a point in is fighting.

I was always ready to meet the challenge, but then Mom decided it was time to split my brother and me up. We had both become avid wrestlers, and she didn't want us meeting each other in competition on opposite sides of the mat, so my brother stayed out there in the country, and I moved back into Salem where I lived once again with my grandparents.

I now have a master's degree of my own. But that didn't come straightaway. There was a break after I graduated high school in 2000, when instead of being in education I was, mostly, in trouble. I knew about trouble and I knew about prison. My mother never wanted to cut me and my brother off from our father, so we would visit him in prison. The idea that someone you knew would be in prison and that you would go there to visit may not be 'normal' as many people see 'normal,' but it was normal to us. The other thing I'd been around because my biological father was around them was motorcycle clubs. I liked them. I still do. The people you meet in motorcycle clubs are my kind of people. They speak my kind of language and have my kind of thoughts. And let's get this clear: most members of most motorcycle clubs are no different from any other American citizen. Whatever fears middle-class Americans may have when they see a bunch of guys in leathers on Harleys are misplaced. You're no more under threat when they are around than at a bankers' convention—and I can promise you, your money will be a damn sight safer.

I have a very clear memory. I've studied psychology to masters level, and I still don't know what this memory says about me. We were in second grade and my brother punched someone in the face. Why? Well, he said, "I wanted to see if it sounded like it does on TV." My brother and I had always been competitive, and I said, "That's not how you do it. You do it like this." And I punched the poor kid in the face too. What I think I was doing was taking the controlled violence that makes up so much of organized sport and carrying it into real life. It isn't part of my life now, and I don't know why it was then, but that's what it became for several years. My brother and I got into our first really big fight with a bunch of other guys early in junior high, and I was in trouble many times for fighting. In fact, in high school I was suspended for one whole semester for fighting.

Why did I do it? I think it has to do with identity. There were more than seven billion people on this planet at the time (there are eight billion now), and it's very easy when you're surrounded by that many to think you are completely insignificant. One of the most important tasks the young have to do is to establish who they are. What position they have in life and in the world. Their identity. I became known as a fighter and my attitude was, "I want to be known for something. I want to stand out. I want a reputation. If fighting is the way to get one, I'll fight." But I got a reputation for something else, too, and in many people's minds the something else was connected with fighting (although it didn't have to be), which possibly made things worse.

Throughout my junior high and high school years, my aunt would take me and my brother to live with her for a month to give my mom a break. My aunt was a couple years older than Mom, and something of a hippie. She was into art and she was into music and the kind of music she introduced my brother and me to was punk rock–The Clash, The Sex Pistols, bands like that. I took to it full on; it affected how I looked as well as what I listened to. I became a skinhead. I didn't know I was a skinhead until someone used that word as an insult, but that's what identity and reputation are about. It isn't what you think you are; it's what other people think. And what other people think can land you in deep trouble. Until you grow up enough to know you have options, it can get you to a place where you think fighting is the only way.

I shaved my head and dressed the way I dressed because it gave me an identity that I liked. I didn't understand any of the political aspects to punk rock and skinheads, but other people did. I spent my first year or so of junior high and my brother spent all of his in a country area, but I moved to Salem, Oregon for high school and Salem was known for the number of white supremacists it nurtured. They called themselves the Volksfront and, to them, having a skinhead in school was no different from having a chapter of the Black Panthers. One day I went to school wearing a Dead Kennedys T-shirt and it got me beaten up. These were big guys, some had even left school, and people were scared of them. While they were pushing me around, they were calling me a SHARP. I'd never heard that expression, so I looked it up. SHARPs were Skinheads Against Racial Prejudice (because not all skinheads were anti-racist, far from it) and I thought, *Well, if that's what they think I am, that's what I'll be.* And I got into that whole anti-racist scene. Looking back, I can see it was a "Fuck you" gesture in the direction of the white supremacists who'd given me such a beating, but that's not how it felt at the time. And there was the gang thing–I was a Rose City Bovver Boys (RCBB) hang around, but they wouldn't let you be a member when you were as young as I was, so a bunch of us formed our own little sub-group called the Capital City Hooligans. If you wanted to be part of a gang, you couldn't just wear the uniform, you had to do something. And the something we did was fight. We'd turn up at neo-Nazi rallies and put the opposing point of view. Forcibly.

Both Capitol City Hooligans and Rose City Bovver Boys did traditional gang jump-ins, where you stood in a circle and were attacked by all members while attempting to fight back. Violence was also used as discipline, and you could be beaten up for minor things like how you dressed, being late, and not following through on commitments. Major discretions such as cooperating with law enforcement, being a coward and not backing up a member, or sleeping with a member's girl would get you jumped out. That was the most severe and most brutal of the three, but even jump-ins would sometimes end with members in hospital.

Starting the Capitol City Hooligans gave me my first real feeling of power. It wasn't long before I realized the fear a group of individuals willing to commit violence could generate. If we weren't invited to a house party (and I wouldn't have invited us, either), we would simply walk in uninvited. Very few people told us to leave and those few regretted it. Eventually, we started using this power to take advantage of young and inexperienced marijuana dealers. We would find out who was selling weed at the different high schools, get connected with them and say we would want a few pounds, and when they would show up with the weed, we would simply take it and walk away without paying. This is how we paid for gas and concert tickets.

The other thing I now realize is how often those who are trying to be like someone else (in our case like Rose City), are often more dangerous than those they imitate. We tried so hard to be like them that we often took it farther than they usually did. Our running battle with the Cherry City Skins also taught me about warfare and the tactical advantage you get when you catch the other side by surprise, so we gathered intel on them. We tried to learn where each member lived, where they worked, what their schedule was, and where they hung out. If we had their schedule, we could look for vulnerable points to attack when they would not be expecting it. This was pre-Internet so intelligence gathering wasn't as easy as it is now, and the wrong information could get innocent people hurt. When Lil Zac was jumped by Volksfront, our Samoan friends asked where the attackers lived. Lil Zac did his best to give them directions and the Samoans came back victorious and happy to tell us about a job well-done. Unfortunately, we later learned that the guys they had drug off their front porch and beaten in retaliation were just some poor dudes in the wrong place at the wrong time, one block over from where the Volksfront house was.

We had a hang around who we didn't really think had what it took to join, but he was persistent and said he would do whatever it took, so I told him to go undercover and join the Cherry City crew. He made friends with them, spent time with them, and eventually was made an official member of their crew, which meant he could tell us where every member lived, worked, and hung out. They weren't too happy when he came back to hanging out with us. Both the information and experience paid off for us. For him, less so.

Lil Zac and I took this information and decided the quickest way to end this beef was to make an example of their leader, Lucas. We got a gun from our Soman friends and sat in some bushes outside of Lucas' apartment. It was dark, but the blinds were open, and Lucas was walking around in front of a big sliding glass door. We were lining up the shot when we saw his young daughter in the room with him. We hadn't planned to kill him—it was more about making a statement, letting them know they could be touched at home. But when we saw the daughter there with him, we aborted the whole thing and, as life works out, I'm glad we did. Formidable enemies for many years, Lucas and I later realized how much we had in common. We became good friends. Lucas even joined the Mongols, as did Lil

Zac. (Yes, I know I haven't mentioned the Mongols before. I will. Oh, yes, I will.) Neither of them is a member today, but we spent a lot of time together after that attempt and have become very close friends. Over the years, I think it's safe to say I learned more from unsuccessful missions than successful ones. The lessons I learned in Capitol City transferred over to Rose City and proved very helpful in my early years in the biker world.

When I was sixteen, I got my first juvenile felony sentence—three years of supervised probation for fighting. That wasn't actually a battle against white supremacists; it was just a fight. A guy in high school, Rob, was bad mouthing a Capital City hooligan. Rob didn't go to school much, but he would meet his friends after school at the bus stop at the bottom of the hill the school sat on where the smokers and stoners usually hung out. Jay and I walked to the bottom of the hill to confront him. A crowd always gathered when there was going to be a fight, and it did here. Approaching the bus stop, Jay and I split up. He went toward Rob and I went up the hill a little ways in case he tried to run. Jay walked up and hit Rob, and Rob ran, right at me. I hit him with all I had. One punch. I don't know if it was the force of the punch or the fact he was running up hill as I was coming down hill, but the blow knocked Rob out. An ambulance took him to the local hospital, and he needed reconstructive surgery as that one punch had caved in his sinus cavity. He told the police what had happened, which broke every rule we were supposed to have, but in any case, everyone at school was talking about it, and next day I was taken out of class by the school resource officer and arrested. So that was a felony assault on my juvenile record.

Then I got a misdemeanor, and that really was for beating up a white power guy. Looking back (isn't hindsight wonderful?), I wonder whether he was really any more a Nazi than I was a skinhead. Maybe–probably–he was one more guy just like me trying to establish an identity for himself.

I was on juvenile probation. I was lifting weights and doing community service, cutting lawns and splitting wood at the juvenile detention center. I was also taking anger management classes. I was on the Scared Straight program for which I had to tour a prison and take a class about the impact of violence. All of that should have done some good, but because I thought I was an activist and the violence I was committing was justified, it didn't. I still pushed my limits with the law. One day I went to pick my brother up from school after detention and ran into Matt Adamson, a Nazi skinhead. As soon as he saw me, he ran. I didn't think much of it, but when Jeremy and I were walking to the car, Matt pulled his truck up next to us and jumped out with a baseball bat. I said, "What do you think you're going to do with that?" and he answered by knocking me to the ground with it. Jeremy charged him and got the same treatment. Matt drove off as some teachers were coming out. They asked us what happened, but we wouldn't talk and we left before the cops got there. A few days later, I rounded up some of the Capitol City Hooligans and went looking for Matt in my grandfather's car. When he pulled into a grocery store parking lot, we jumped him. We had done him some serious damage when the sound of sirens told us to get out of there.

A few days later, my probation officer called and told me I needed to come see her about the incident. My grandfather sat me down and talked to me about it, and he wanted to take me to see her and do the right thing and turn myself in. I told him I was going to run and had already packed a bag. That was one of the few times I ever saw my grandfather cry. He was such a tough man, WWII vet, army boxing champion, but me running broke his heart. It was hard to watch and I don't think I'll ever forget it. Jeremy, Jay, and I took a Greyhound bus to Eugene, Oregon. While there, we went to a concert; it was Dropkick Murphys and The Ducky Boys. The Dropkick Murphys wasn't a well-known band back then, and it was a small venue. We spent time with the band after the show. When we told them we were on the run, they suggested we follow their tour, so we took a bus to the next show in Portland and then went on to Seattle. It took about a week for Jay and Jeremy to decide to go home, but I stayed in Portland for another week or two. Then it turned out that Matt was also on probation, and he pursued charges it could come up that he'd attacked us first, so he decided not to press charges. My warrant was rescinded, and I went back to live with my grandparents.

Then I turned eighteen, which is when the law gets serious, and a month after my birthday, I caught a felony charge. The result of all this was that I spent a great deal of my time between the ages of sixteen and thirty either in and out of jail or on probation. And what I know now, though I didn't know then, is that, once you're in the system, you're in it. Getting out is very difficult. The police know you as a troublemaker, and when they need a body, they come looking for you. That experience–that knowledge of just how hard it is to get out of the system once you're in it–is a lot of what fuels me now as a social worker. I don't blame the cops; I understand why they make the assumptions they do, but I can tell you: lifting yourself out of the net is one of the hardest things you can do.

By 2008, I was beginning to realize I'd gotten myself into a dead end. I went back to school. I had had five years of supervised probation; one of the stipulations was that I wasn't allowed to have any contact with the club I'd been in. If I was caught hanging out with them–any of them–I was back in jail. And I got caught a lot because, although we didn't know it, we had a number of paid confidential informants embedded with us. The police must have thought we were hilarious–we were acting this tough lifestyle in defiance of society and its norms, and we didn't even understand that some of these guys we would trust with our lives were, in fact, informants. We had these secret conversations, which immediately became known to every cop in the neighborhood. I'd have a month or two on the outside, then a month or two in jail. It became a second home; I had what I started to think of as my own cell. I got to know the guards quite well, and one day, one of them pulled me aside. He said, "Hey, man, you lost me a bet."

"Me?"

"You. I thought I had you figured out. I said you wouldn't be coming back here again. I put money on it. But here you are."

I told myself I didn't know why he would think that, but I did. All I had to do was look around. These guys, just as regular in this place as me, they were into drugs, they didn't think about anything except right now, and if I let myself, I knew what the guard was telling me. This wasn't me. I thought of myself as an intelligent, well-spoken guy, I had a lot of friends; I was living a life that wasn't the life I was designed for. And why was I in here? Aside from hanging out with the club, I wasn't breaking the law, I wasn't doing anything wrong. The guard was right. I needed to make some changes. I needed to do something different with my life. And I could think about all kinds of changes, but they all involved getting an education. Without that, all I was ever going to have was dreams.

There was a guy I knew in the club who was about as tough as anyone I ever met, but he had a PhD in psychology. I looked at him and I thought, *If he can do it, I can do it.* I started with an associate's degree in drug and alcohol counseling. There were two reasons for that: I saw counseling as part of my future, and it was something I could do with a felony. That matters because, when you're a young guy and you're happily indulging in the kind of activity that ends with a felony charge, you don't realize at the time that you are closing doors. There are things you might want to do for which you need to be qualified and the simple fact of having a felony in your history means you will never be allowed to get that qualification. So that's how I began, but I fell in love with psychology and went on to graduate with a full bachelor's degree in psychology, and then I did my master's in social work.

My criminal record was largely about violence. I had convinced myself that I was some kind of social warrior and that was nonsense.

What I was really about was establishing a personality, and I had chosen the wrong one. Violence doesn't achieve very much, and what it does achieve is never good. And I knew that because whenever I have really hurt someone, I had regretted it. I had felt for that other person. And now I'd accepted that I had to do things differently and I did. That spell in jail, when the guard told me I'd caused him to lose a bet, was my last. I walked out of there and registered for college, and although I remained on probation for a number of years, I was never in jail again. That doesn't mean I was without opportunities to offend. I went on being a member of a pretty violent motorcycle club, and if I'd wanted to get into trouble, it would not have been difficult. But something had happened inside my head. I knew I wanted to get off the road I was traveling because I knew it didn't lead anywhere except to a dead end (perhaps literally). And I did. I don't know who it was who first said, "If you don't like your life, you can change it," but they were right.

CHAPTER TWO

WHEN I LOOK BACK on those teenage and new adult years, what I think about most is my mother and what we put her through. Raising twins is never going to be easy, but it didn't have to be as bad as we made it. Even before that, when we were small and needed babysitters, we would terrorize them in an attempt–usually successful–to get them to quit. We'd run around in our underwear, shooting pellet guns at each other and at them. Eventually, they took our pellet guns away, but before that, they just hid the pellets. We soon learned that tapioca balls worked just as well. After I'd shot at Jeremy point blank and lodged a tapioca ball deep in his back, they took our pellet guns away too.

Then there was the time in the sixth grade that we attempted to make a ChapStick bomb in our bedroom. We filled a ChapStick container up with black powder, wrapped it tight, and then realized we'd forgotten to make a hole for the wick, so we heated a needle and stuck it in the side of the container. Jeremy had to go to the hospital to have plastic pieces shaved from his eyeball.

A year later, Jeremy had filled a sock with golf balls and was beating me with it. He said he was going to take some of my Halloween candy and said there was nothing I could do about it, so I grabbed a pair of sewing scissors and told him if he tried, I was going to stab him. Well, I guess he didn't believe me, and I was tired of getting hit, so I chucked the scissors at him. They buried themselves in his thigh right up to the handle. I remember a weird silence as we both processed what had happened. Jeremy said, "I am going to tell Mom."

"You'd better not, just take them out and go to bed." He decided, probably rightly, that it was time to get an adult's view; when Mom looked at his leg, the look on her face was pure disgust.

She called our stepdad into the room. "I don't want to take him to the doctor. We've just got over the plastic on his eyeballs. The doctor will think we are dysfunctional." So my stepdad removed the scissors and then used bandages and superglue to fix the problem, which, amazingly, it did, though Jeremy walked with a limp for a few weeks.

At some point, our parents thought maybe we would stop shooting shit at each other if we learned to respect firearms, so they enrolled us in a hunter's safety class. We were kicked out for throwing rocks at another student.

It didn't get any better, and I guess, as well as regretting the impact on our mother, I thought we should be thinking about how our neighbors felt about what was going on. Sometime in high school, we were out driving in the country, Jeremy with a carload of friends in the Honda Civic he had gotten as his first car and me as passenger in a pickup truck behind him. As we came to a stop sign, a pump air rifle slid out from under the seat. I didn't even think about it. I picked it up, pumped it about twenty times, and took a shot at Jeremy's car. Both vehicles were moving, and I thought a car's back window would be too strong for a pellet gun to break it. I was wrong. His rear window shattered. When he saw me doubled over laughing, he chased me around the truck with a baseball bat.

It wasn't all bad. When Grandpa decided it was time for me to get a job, he drove me from place to place and went in with me. I was into photography in high school and my first job was at a camera retailer called The Shutterbug. They said they hired me because I was the first candidate to have their grandpa come in and vouch for them.

Grandpa always had a couple of cars, and he used to loan me the Chrysler LeBaron. Jeremy got his driver's license before me, and my parents helped him get a car. It took me longer to get mine, and because Grandpa had a few cars, they figured I didn't need my own car and could just take his when I needed it. The first time we got to drive the LeBaron, Jeremy had just gotten his driver's license. We were cruising around with nothing to do, so we decided we would stop by this pizza place on the west side of town where a member of a rival skinhead gang, Cherry City Skinheads, worked. He wasn't there, and we were headed home when he pulled up beside us at a red light in the middle of downtown Salem. He jumped out of his car yelling, "I heard you guys were looking for me. Well, here I am." He walked up to the car and kicked the back window with his Doc Martin boots, and the rear passenger window shattered. Jeremy put the car in park, grabbed the brass knuckles he had resting on the dash, and went to work on this dude. We were downtown in the middle of the road. Cars were honking, we could hear sirens in the distance, and I was yelling that we needed to go. I was on probation and didn't want to be there when the cops arrived. We left a bloodied skinhead on the side of the road, and Grandpa's passenger window in pieces all over the asphalt.

One weekend, while staying the night at a friend's house, I got the idea it would be cool to drive on acid. We hadn't taken much, so we thought, and we decided we wanted to go get some more. We didn't even make it out of the driveway. While backing up and turning to get out of the driveway, I ended up overshooting the road and sideswiping a tree. I believe we told Grandpa someone hit it overnight, but I doubt he believed us. This poor LeBaron took a lot of damage because of us, and the last time we wrecked it, he sent it to the junkyard. It was a gloomy and rainy day in Portland. I had driven up to visit Jeremy who was living near Union Station. We were driving around Portland during five o'clock stop and go traffic. A few weeks prior, we had bought a handheld cattle prod. We were sneaking it into concerts and using it against anyone we perceived as enemies at the time, but we also were using it on each other as a form of entertainment. One time while staying the night at Jeremy's Union Station apartments, he was asleep with his foot sticking off the bed. I thought this was a great chance to see what this cattle prod could do, and I zapped his foot with it. He was pissed, and obviously waiting for his chance to get me back. So, on this gloomy rainy day, at the height of peak city traffic, he decided to stick the cattle prod in my neck as I was crossing the Burnside Bridge. He didn't actually shock me with it, but he kept holding it up to my neck and threatening to. I was so distracted looking at him and trying not to get tazed in the throat that I didn't realize traffic had come to a stop, and I rammed into the car in front of me. Thankfully, no one was hurt, but the poor LeBaron didn't make it. Now, I didn't want to snitch on Jeremy, so I never told my family about the cattle prod. And once Jeremy was convinced I wasn't going to tell, he liked to bring up at family gatherings how ol' Justin just wasn't paying attention to the road and what lesson this might serve as. Honestly, I don't think my parents know about the cattle prod even now.

I've said I think a lot about our poor mom, but let's not leave Grandpa out of this. I caused him a lot of grief. I was getting into trouble, and he couldn't see any direction in my life. He was right. At the time I had no idea what I wanted to do. During my junior year of high school, I got a call from an air force recruiter. Grandpa had been in the army and served in the Pacific during World War II. He was still in high school when he got sent off to war. He had decided I needed some structure in my life and called an air force recruiter. I told the recruiter I wasn't interested, but I did spend some time talking with Grandpa about it. At the time, my very best friend, Petey, was in the Marine Corps delayed entry program. I started to get excited about it and was spending more and more time meeting with the Marine Corps recruiter, but my felony in the summer of 1999 meant I was no longer eligible to join. Petey went on to join and is still active in the military to this day. I decided that the military wasn't for me and moved forward with gang life. I did try to join the military again around 2005. My band, The Escaped, was breaking up, I was growing out of the skinhead scene, and once again trying to figure out what I wanted to do with my life. I met with every branch of the military, as many of the recruitment standards had relaxed and having a felony no longer meant immediate disqualification. By now, though, I had a lot of visible tattoos, some on my neck and hands, and no branch would allow me to join with neck and hand tattoos. I joined a program that helped gang-affected youth remove their tattoos and went to two sessions to have the tattoos on the side of my neck removed. It was ridiculously painful. Because this was a nonprofit program, it used volunteers and donated equipment, and the laser removal machine they had at that time couldn't remove colored ink, so I only attempted to remove the tattoos on my neck and not the one on my hand since it had color in it. I had an army national guard recruiter that was convinced he could get the proper waivers to get me in. I even introduced one of our band's singers to this recruiter, and my childhood friend, Luke, who was in the Capital City Hooligans with us, and was also on my high school wrestling team. Luke and our singer, Carter, got in, and I did not. The recruiter could not get the waivers he needed for my tattoos and I was told I could not join. Luke and Carter are still in the army to this day. The military just wasn't in the cards for me.

CHAPTER THREE

BY THE TIME I was twenty-eight, a lot of people would say I'd wasted most of the time since arriving in Portland aged eighteen, but that isn't how I saw it. I thought the stuff I'd learned–about me, about life, about the world–had been worth it. But then, at twenty-eight, I started to get my life together. Right now I was twenty-four, and before I got to be twenty-five, I would attempt to bring my life to an end.

My 1999 felony assault conviction had gotten me ten days in jail during the Christmas break in my senior year, and after graduation, I'd had to turn myself in for another thirty days jail time. When I got out, a number of us moved to Portland–me, Jeremy, Luke from the Capital City Hooligans, and Lil Zac, who'd been on my high school wrestling team, as well as Nate, who had gotten me into punk rock in the first place. I got a job at The Hot Topic where anyone with an interest in counterculture and the music of the day was likely to show up. That's where I met Zac Fishnets, so called because of the rocker-style fishnet shirts he wore. After becoming part of the motorcycle club world, I remember once describing Zac as a 'sweet dude,' and being told, "We don't use expressions like sweet dude around here."

I already had a band and I invited Zac to play in it. I didn't get the feeling Zac had huge respect for my band; in any case, he asked if I wouldn't rather start a band with him. And that's what we did. We called the band The Escaped, and we had some success, but what we had a lot more of was enjoyment. Wasting my time? I don't think so.

I came close to making a mistake of the most serious kind in 2001 at a Misfits Concert in Portland when Volksfront members who had bullied me in high school showed up. Rose City Bovver Boys were there in force and we waited outside until the Volksfront left. We attacked them right there, in the street in the middle of downtown with ordinary citizens all around. When I saw Tony, their leader, a flash of rage came over me. All of those years as a bully and as an enemy, and here he was in front of me. I pulled my knife from my pocket and unfolded it. That was how close I came. I thank whatever gods there may be that I came to my senses. It was like something in a movie. I looked around, just the way the movie camera does. Did I experience total silence, or was there mood music playing? I don't remember, but I do remember it was like watching something in the theater and not as something that happened in real life. I saw bodies lying in the street and RCBB standing over them. But what I also saw was the wide eyes of people at the restaurant across the street. They were at patio tables, and they were staring in horror. Most important, they were witnesses. I folded my knife back in my pocket and the scene went back from the movie set to everyday life. I yelled for everyone to leave. As we were leaving, one of the Volksfront members was staggering to his feet, and I hit him as hard as I could, all of my years of anger in one punch, and I felt the sharp pain of my hand breaking as it connected with his head.

The police were so close that we passed them as they were setting up a perimeter. I never came closer than that to writing off my whole life and I learned a valuable lesson about rage and the desire for revenge and how they can fuck up your whole future. It's a lesson I hope I've passed on to others in my later life. And I drew another lesson. I could have committed murder—and what would have let me do that was the fact that I was carrying a knife. If you're not carrying a knife, you can't stab anyone, which means you can't risk spending your whole life in prison.

There were rules about how people who operated on the fringes of the law–people like Rose City Bovver Boys and members of Volksfront–conducted themselves. One was that you never–ever–snitched to the law. We were shocked when the Volksfront members broke that law. They cooperated with law enforcement and told the Portland PD that Justin and Jeremy DeLoretto had attacked them because they belonged to Volksfront. Jeremy and I were asked to come in to the Portland police department for questioning. Instead, we hired an attorney. Our attorney brought witness statements from several concert goers who said they had witnessed us leaving before the fight. In the end, it was our word against the word of a neo-Nazi group in liberal Portland. No charges were filed.

Now that tour. I said it might cause people to question my common sense, but to me and Zac at the time, it seemed the obvious thing to do. We had a band. America liked bands. So we'd take our band to America. ALL of America. We'd been a band for less than a year but, because we were young and superintelligent, we let our drummer fix up a 1980s Econoline which, on the very first day of the tour, broke down between Portland and Medford.

We soldiered on. We did the Medford concert, we played Northern California, we kept fixing up the Ford and moving on to the next date and then the next. Our van broke down right outside of Compton, after dark. California Highway Patrol doesn't like cars on the side of the freeway, so they towed us off at the next exit, which was Compton. Here we were, white kids with shaved heads and colored hair, walking the streets of Compton, looking for an auto parts store to get a new battery. We ended up making it to the show and played with an East LA band called Union 13. That was the best show of the tour and a huge culture shock for white middle-class kids from Oregon.

And then came Texas. We were met pretty well on the state border by the ever-welcoming Texas State Police whose hospitality is famous worldwide. Naturally, they were concerned by the sight of punk rockers with dyed hair, and we were all frisked to ensure there would be no risk to the innocence of the Lone Star State's residents. Then they took everything out of the van, checked it over, and left. By the time we'd got it all back into the van, it was touch and go whether we'd reach Austin in time for that night's performance but, as it turned out, with thirty minutes still to go to the city line, the van caught fire and burned out.

We were supposed to play with Complete Control and the Krum Bums that night and they were just great. All my experience with musicians and bands has been good—I have nothing but happy memories of time spent with them, and that experience in Austin was typical. They opened up their homes for us, put us up, fed us, looked after the other needs wandering minstrels are subject to, and those guys remain my friends today.

I ended up staying in Austin for about two months, though Zac had gone to Connecticut for reasons that now escape me, and the rest of the band drifted away. We had no money to get home, and we didn't have jobs, so we'd join in with local bands and use the money they gave us to get our boys the bus fare home one at a time until there was only me left. Finally, I was able to afford two and a half days on a Greyhound bus from Austin back to Portland and our first American tour adventure was over. But not our existence as a band. We spent four more years on the road after that, playing famous places like CBGBs in New York City and Gilman Street in the Bay Area. We did some WARPED tour dates, playing outside the Rock & Roll Hall of Fame in Cleveland, and did a Canadian tour.

I can summarize what had been going on by saying that I learned street combat with the Capital City Hooligans, and I refined it with Rose City Bovver Boys. I was also, with the Bovver Boys, going from being one of the crew to working my way up toward a position of leadership. At the same time, I was in the band and the band was touring, so I met other gangs in other cities and made a lot of connections. There's a limit to what those connections give you, but at the time I didn't know that. I would learn.

Los Angeles had Unity Skins and Carson Skins, the Bay Area had OBHC (Oakland Brand Hard Core) and Most Hated, and even Seattle was starting to get a crew together. What we thought we were doing was building a network and getting everyone on the same page. Not for criminal reasons—more for bands to play back and forth with each other, coordinate parties, and have some way of settling issues that arose with other crews. The most obvious example was Integrity from Cleveland, Ohio. They'd been around for a long time. I don't actually remember who made the call, but I believe it was OBHC who first reached out and said they didn't want Integrity playing on the West Coast. There were issues around racist stuff the drummer had spouted on stage, and this was our first chance to show that we really could work together and do things together. Integrity had planned to play in LA and a big group of guys went there and told them it just wasn't going to happen. The same thing happened in the Bay Area. By the time word reached us in Portland, Integrity were already about to go on stage.

This was a pivotal point for me in the leadership of Rose City. Some of the older guys who'd been running things were ready to step aside for younger blood. Now I had a chance to show those older guys that I was able to call the shots and put something together. On top of that, I wanted to show the other gangs that we weren't just their equals; we were probably ready to go to higher levels than they were. So, unlike the others, we didn't warn them off and tell them they couldn't play in Portland. Instead, we waited until the concert had started, and then we attacked them on stage. We beat them up onstage and off it, we took their equipment, we canceled their concert.

We had sent a message. In fact, we'd sent two. The first was to Integrity and it was simple enough: You are not welcome here. The second was more important than that because it was to other groups and gangs. We didn't yet have the kind of social media we have today, but there were online news groups and message boards and we were being talked about. People were finding out who we were, what we were about, and how we operated.

The next step in our progress (and my progress in particular), involved a successful hardcore band out of New York with a close connection to the DMS Crew. I had a lot of respect for that band; in fact, you could say I looked up to them. We would hang out with some of their members when both bands were touring in the same place. We got along. They'd had issues of their own with Integrity, so they were fully in support of the actions we'd taken. But isn't it strange how so many things that go wrong turn out to be about a girl?

I was in my first serious relationship. It lasted five years. She was in a contest; in the end, she didn't win, but she went a long way before losing out and part of that involved a trip to New York. She asked me where she should go while she was there, and I suggested the name of a bar on the Lower East side where the DMS band hung out. Why not? We were friends with the band so I could rely on them to look out for her. Couldn't I? And then I learned they may have looked out for her too well. Somebody wrote on a message board that Kristin, my girlfriend, had slept with their lead singer, who was also the half-brother of a vocalist who had founded one of American punk's foremost bands at the beginning of the 1980s.

I wasn't green enough to assume that something on a message board was true. I tried to call the singer, and he either wouldn't or didn't answer. I reached out to other members of the band, and they wouldn't answer either. I wasn't at that point looking for a fight. What I wanted was to know what had been going on. I talked to Kristin and she said she'd been raped. Now, I didn't assume immediately that that was true—it's something that other women have said when they find themselves having to explain a sex act and it isn't always true, but at least now I knew there had been a sex act. That would have been a betrayal in itself, but if the singer really had raped her, I'd consider that serious. So would anyone else, in my opinion.

The DMS guys made their position clear. The singer was married, his wife must not hear about the rape allegation, I had better drop the subject. I told them, "I just want to hear from him man-to-man. I want to hear his side of the story. Get him to call me. If you can't do that, get him to take my calls." I thought I was due that as a matter of simple respect, but the response was not positive: "Leave it alone. If you keep pushing this, someone's gonna get hurt. It could be you."

And then I found that mutual friends were backing away from me. Really, I should have expected that. The DMS band was bigger than us, DMS themselves had great power, and if a band had to choose between a gig with us and a gig with them, we would not be the best choice. But for me, what was at issue here was a simple matter of honor. The band's lead and I were friends, or so I had believed, and this was not how one friend behaved toward another.

This went on for a while. People who were going to help bring out our band's single backed away. So did people who had promised to help in other ways. But some friends remained. I reached out several times to the DMS band and was blown off each time, so in the end, I decided we had to make a stand. I knew they were planning a big tour, and I told them they couldn't play in our area. Then I started using the reconnaissance skills I'd developed.

Their tour began in Boise, Idaho and I had friends there just watching. Were they mob-handed, with a lot of people over and above band members? Did they have security? Who helped them unload and load? As the tour went on, more intel came in. And when they were performing in Seattle, we already knew a lot about them. We'd identified weak spots. Next stop, Portland. There's only one interstate into Portland, and Jeremy parked his motorcycle by the side of it as though he had broken down. He waited until the DMS band's van passed and fell in behind it, radioing ahead to let us know they were on their way.

We got our people in position in advance, with some guys who were carrying waiting in the background–they would only get involved if the other side was armed and looked like using their armament. Jeremy kept us in touch with progress so we always knew where they were. When they pulled into the venue, it probably looked to them like a bunch of people milling around waiting for the concert to start, but as soon as they stopped, we opened the van doors and started pulling them out and beating them up. Something that has always amused me about that was that this was really all about one man–the lead singer–and that man locked himself in the van. Of course, everyone has to follow their own guiding star, and I've no doubt that he had and has his, but in the world I inhabited at the time, 'classy' was not how we would describe the behavior of someone who had provoked a fight and then watched other people having the shit beaten out of them. Actually, it still isn't.

We had this well enough planned that there had been no surveillance and, when the cops showed up, we were gone. And there wasn't any doubt, we were seen as hometown heroes. But we'd also created problems for ourselves. Unity and Carson stayed neutral; every other group and crew that had promised us support started to back away when they saw the scale of what had happened. And you can understand why. If you had a band, you could do great business, as long as you stayed near Portland. If you wanted to tour and you supported us, DMS made it clear that they would do to you what we had done to their guys.

The older guys in Rose City decided they wanted to calm things down. The DMS lead singer's older half-brother was due to perform in Portland in two months' time with his new band. The plan was that Jeremy as my brother and he as the lead singer's brother should sit down together and talk. That was what we were told; they would talk. With any luck, they'd work out some way to defuse the situation.

So Jeremy went. But as it turned out, the only side that thought the meeting was to talk was ours. DMS had brought a gang of guys not just from DMS but also from Most Hated, OBHC, and FSU, and they beat Jeremy so hard they almost killed him. They broke his jaw and ripped off an ear. He was leaking brain fluid. He spent two weeks in ICU and he suffered some serious issues for a long time. In fact, he still does; he's 100 percent deaf in the ear that was torn off, and he still gets serious migraines and night sweats from the brain damage he suffered.

The lead singer's older brother had a cancer operation in 2021 from which I believe he is still recovering. He racked up some pretty alarming medical bills, and a GoFundMe page was started to allow punk rock fans to 'show the love' by helping him pay. With my brother around as a perpetual reminder of the love he himself had shown, I'm afraid I couldn't bring myself to contribute.

Then some senior Rose City guys–the ones who'd arranged the so-called talking session at which my brother had suffered life-changing damage–turned up. They handed me a firearm and told me to "go take care of it."

All of this was at the root of my band's breakup. We couldn't tour outside our own area because of the threats against us, and those who had distributed our records were told to choose between us and DMS. Most chose DMS. But it was also the beginning of the end of my time as a gang member.

Lil Zac and I were at a meeting with some older guys to talk about putting plans into action. The older guys had brought a pillowcase full of pistols, which they tipped onto the table. "You guys have to go to Sacramento with these and put things right. You have to show them that Rose City Bovver Boys is not a gang that takes things lightly. They have to learn, 'You fuck with us, we fuck with you.'"

I said, "When do we leave?" And the answer was: "We're not leaving. You and Zac are going."

I went home and my head was spinning. I talked to Zac and he was all set; he wanted vengeance for Jeremy just like I did. And then we told Jeremy and he was pissed. "So I get beaten half to death and you guys end up dead or in prison. That's supposed to be revenge? How does that work?"

The question we wrestled with then was, If we are doing this on our own, what's the point of being in a gang? We regarded the gang as the next closest thing to family, and we'd been fooling ourselves. Not all, but some of the older guys had made it clear that the only thing that mattered to them was maintaining RCBB's name. If two of the younger members–me and Zac–ended up dead or doing life, that would do the reputation no harm. Did we matter? Not for ourselves, we didn't. If we mattered, we mattered only as a way to enhance their reputation.

A lot of things came together now. I took a good look at the life I'd been leading and it troubled me. I began this chapter by saying that I didn't think I'd been wasting my life and I don't, but that wasn't how I felt then. I was twenty-four years old. I'd tried to get into the army and failed. I knew I had a good brain and, even though I came from a family of teachers, I'd done nothing with it. I had devoted a big chunk of my life to a gang that I believed valued me as a person and I now knew that–as a person–I didn't matter at all. People I'd regarded as friends had turned out not to be. And now my band couldn't tour and was breaking up. I had a felony record I couldn't get rid of and I had no career. I'd spent the last five years managing an adult video store, and you can't make a lifetime career out of selling porn. When I was young, I hadn't known how to handle credit, and now I was going through a bankruptcy. My mental health wasn't good. I no longer believed in what we were doing as a band; we had fans, but I thought they liked us as people and not for our music. Kristin had been my first serious relationship, and we had broken up.

It all came to a head one night. Kristin was still living with me, even though we had broken up. We'd been fighting for days. I had taken a break and told her I was going to go get some food; instead, I bought two hundred sleeping pills and one Gatorade. Thinking back later, I would be shocked that no one raised an eyebrow when I bought that quantity of pills, but all I was thinking of then was getting it over with. I sat in our band's van in front of our apartment and thought things over one last time. The I took handfuls of pills at a time and washed them down with the Gatorade until the bottle was empty. I thought, *This is it. There's no going back from here.* I went inside. I told Kristin I loved her, held her tight, and went to sleep, not expecting to wake ever again. If she hadn't been there, I don't suppose I would have, but I was throwing up in my sleep, and Kristin kept trying to wake me to find out what was wrong. When she finally accepted she wasn't going to be able to, she called 911.

I did wake up and it was in the hospital. They cleaned me out and I spent the next five or so days in a mental hospital being assessed. They put me on antidepressants and turned me out to restart my life. And that's what I did. If life really resembles art and you can see it as a three act play, I had just reached the end of Act One. Therapists will tell you that you can't help someone until they hit rock bottom. Usually when they say that, they're talking about alcoholics, but I've never been much of a drinker and I hadn't at that time touched drugs and I'm here to tell you that it's far more widely applicable than that.

And I can also tell you that after you hit rock bottom, there's only one way to go—up. In my case, after leaving a gang that existed only to fight and getting into the motorcycle club scene.

CHAPTER FOUR

I SHOULD HAVE FELT AT home with motorcycles—my father and stepfather were both riders. Like most kids growing up in the 1990s, I rode my Huffy bicycle to school and spent what was left of the day after school riding around with friends until the sun went down. And that hasn't changed much. I'm still riding bikes with my friends, but my curfew extends a bit longer and the bikes have a lot more power. My grandpa and stepdad taught me how to ride a bicycle; it was my biological dad who tried to teach me how to ride a motorcycle. My first attempt took place in his backyard on a two-stroke Yamaha dirt bike. He was teaching me how the clutch worked, and once he thought I had it down, he sent me off on my own. I remember the adrenaline as the motor idled, and I worked up the nerve to pull back the throttle and kick it into gear. I ended up grabbing way too much throttle and the front wheel popped right up, knocking me back on the seat. Once it came down, I froze in a panic, burned my right calf on the exhaust pipe, barreled straight through some blackberry bushes, and stopped when I crashed into the neighbor's fence.

My second attempt was on my stepfather's farm but otherwise not much different. It was on an old two-stroke Hodaka Super Rat. I did a little better starting off the second time, although once I hit the two-stroke's power band, the same thing happened. This time, once the front wheel came down, I was doing my best Superman impression as I hung off the back of the bike until, again, a fence put an end to my ride.

Vintage Vespa scooters were popular in the skinhead scene. A few older Bovver Boys rode sport bikes and café style bikes, but most preferred scooters. Jeremy was the first in our circle to get one, and one day I finally talked him into letting me ride it. I took off down the street without a helmet and thought things were going great. What do they say about someone who makes the same mistake three times? Because that was me. Sitting at a stop sign about to turn left, there was a car coming and I felt pressured to go. So instead of easing into it like I had the first block or two, I grabbed too much throttle, twisted the grip into first gear, and was off, roaring down a sidewalk, feet flailing behind me, with no idea how to get to the foot brake. Before I could figure it out, a car parked halfway in the driveway and half on the sidewalk made sure I came to a complete stop. I woke up in a bush on the other side of the car. Once I realized what had happened, I was trying to flee. Because it was on its side, the Vespa didn't want to kick over, so I started off pushing it down the street and back toward home before the car's owner came out. Jeremy came looking for me since my trip around the block had lasted longer than expected. He took one look at the broken headlight and another at me, covered in bark dust. "Did you crash?"

Of course, I was insulted he would even suggest such a thing and vehemently denied it. However, it didn't take long before my head began to pound, and I ended up going to the hospital due to brain swelling from the crash.

I got my own Vespa shortly after that. It was a little ripper for a vintage two-stroke, a 1963 150 Super, around 180 cc. I didn't have too many accidents after that and my riding skills continued to improve. Because Vespas are over 50 cc, they are classed in Oregon as motorcycles and require a motorcycle license, but most cops didn't know the capacity of a vintage scooter and assumed it was a moped. I went years without a motorcycle license. The only other crash I had on the Vespa was out front of my apartment. I put it on the center stand and was warming it up, idling in the parking lot, when

I grabbed the handlebars and accidently shifted it into gear when I wasn't ready. The scooter shot out from underneath my legs and went straight into the broad side of my neighbor's car. I wasn't able to flee from that one and ended up having to pay to fix their passenger door.

Jeremy, Lil Zac, and I all had scooters by now and we were ripping all over Portland. We would ride to reggae night every Friday and park out front. We decided to ride to a scooter rally in Eugene, about a 120 mile ride. Since our scooters were so lightweight and not fast enough to go on the interstate, we had to find back roads and small highways to get us there. The trip took us a full day, partly because of the route, but a big factor was the sidecar on Lil Zac's Vespa that we had loaded down with beer so he topped out at fifty mph when the rest of us could do closer to seventy. After that trip, we were ready to graduate to motorcycles.

It was Corvallis, Oregon that finally got me off scooters and onto motorcycles. An older skinhead named Joey owned the Sacred Art Tattoo shop there, and I lived with Joey and worked at the shop for a while, scheduling appointments and cleaning. Joey had a Vespa and two Harleys, and one day he asked me if I wanted to ride his Heritage Softail. It felt big and heavy and I was intimidated. The last thing I wanted to do was crash one of his nice Harleys. But he insisted so I finally gave it a shot. At first I just rode around the block a few times, afraid to shift past second gear, but after a few laps, he hopped on his Springer Softail and told me to keep up. It wasn't long before the speedometer needle hit one hundred mph and that was it. I was hooked. I was in my early 20s, I didn't have much established credit, and the credit I did have was less than stellar. I had opened a few gas station credit cards for the band when we toured, and they usually didn't get paid back on time, if at all. The only place that offered me a loan was the Honda dealership, and because I was still a skinhead and not yet into the biker scene, I didn't care that it wasn't a Harley. It was a Shadow 1100, and compared to my Vespa, it ran at warp speed. I fell in love with the torque and power. Lil Zac bought a Yamaha, and Jeremy was working on a deal with Joey for his Heritage. We spent the summer riding those bikes all over and it wasn't long before we all wanted Harleys. Jeremy went into the local Harley dealership and was approved for financing, and being the kind brother he is, he figured we should both get Harleys, so he cosigned for me to get one too. Jeremy and I each got Sportsters. He got an 883 and I got a 1200 custom. Harley salesmen will tell you they love to sell Sportsters because it's a guaranteed two bike sale. It is very common for people to start with the smaller Sportster to learn how to ride and trade it in within a year for a big twin. We were no exception to the rule, getting our first big twins in 2005. Jeremy bought a 2006 Heritage Springer, I got a 2006 Night Train, and Little Zac traded in his Yamaha for a Heritage Softail.

Once the three of us had motorcycles, Fishnets really wanted one too. He had never even ridden a scooter so he had no idea how to ride at all. He bought a used Sportster and I would go over to his house after work and teach him how to ride. For a while it seemed hopeless, but he started to improve, and one night we decided to invite him to join our ride to reggae night. He'd been working on managing the clutch and was still having a hard time making a turn from a stop. It was a slow ride, but we all made it safely, and we parked our Harleys next to a row of Vespas.

Once he had more experience riding, it was time to get him some time in on the interstate. The speed of traffic was much faster there, so we made sure he wore a full face helmet to protect himself. He ended up doing just fine on the interstate; the trouble came as we were trying to find a friend's house. I was up front, leading a group of about four of us, and since Fishnets was the new guy, he was at the back. I recall turning on my right blinker and slowing for a turn when all I heard was screeching brakes; Nets had speeded up and realized too late that I was turning. His front wheel narrowly missed my leg and crashed into the back wheel of my bike. It knocked me over, but the force threw Nets through the air to land on his head and skid down the street on the face of the helmet and the shoulder of his leather jacket. He had one of those punk rock leather jackets covered in spikes and the studs were sparking as he skidded down the street. Thankfully, since he was wearing his helmet, everyone was okay. When his bike was in the shop getting repaired, I had the mechanic cut off the ugly leather fringe on his clutch and brake levers. He was bummed to learn the fringe didn't survive the crash.

Getting into motorcycles changed the entire course of my life. I was twenty-four years old, not long home from the hospital after a suicide attempt. The band had broken up. I wanted to put RCBB and everything connected with it behind me. All I wanted to do was ride. Just like I did with the skinhead stuff, I bought and read every book I could about motorcycles and motorcycle clubs. All I knew about motorcycle clubs before that was from movies and old folklore. Working at the porn store one day, a longtime Rose City member saw me reading "Under and Alone" about an ATF agent who infiltrated a club called The Mongols. There were no Mongols in Oregon, and at the time I had no idea who they were. He said, "Mongols, huh? Some of the guys from Carson Skinheads joined the Mongols." Although that connection didn't mean much to me at the time, it made a lot of sense later on. What I did know was that I was ready to leave the skinhead scene behind, and I wanted to be in a motorcycle club.

When I finally got to college, I majored in social work and psychology, and no one with any grounding in psychology is going to miss the received idea that someone like me, who couldn't wait to join a gang and then couldn't wait to join a motorcycle club, must be looking for a family. I accept that that's the theory and I accept that it's often correct, but not in my case. As I've already made clear, I have since birth been part of a close Italian family and all the "family" things I need, I have. Even during the gang times, even when I was arrested, my family has always been there offering total support. They helped me get bail, get attorneys, whatever I needed, my family was always there for me. What I think I was looking for, first in the gangs and then in the clubs, was identity. I wanted to know who I was and I wanted other people to know it too. Does a twin have a greater need to establish his or her own identity than someone who is not a twin? I have no idea; how many twins do I know, for God's sake? But I do know that it was something I needed. And there was the political angle, the anti-racist angle, which mattered because Portland today has seen a big influx of people from California and now looks very much like a model liberal society, but Portland when I was growing up was deeply racist. I think we saw ourselves as social warriors, fighting (often extremely violently) for a fairer society. And we weren't a street gang; we weren't out there hustling and making money.

It sounds very easy to say I left the Rose City Bovver Boys and joined the Outsiders motorcycle club. In fact, of course, it wasn't straightforward. You don't just leave a skinhead gang and you don't just join a motorcycle club. When I made it clear that I wanted to leave, a number of Bovver Boys had been backing away from me, and it seemed I would just be allowed to leave. But it's a long-standing gang rule that you can't be in two organizations at the same time, and one or two RCBB members, when they found I intended to join a motorcycle club, said I would have to be jumped out. And anyone wanting to join a motorcycle club has to spend some time prospecting, which doesn't mean looking for gold; it means being a prospect so that those who are already members can decide whether you make the grade.

There are many different ideas about prospecting and each club prospects their members in their own way. From the outside looking in, prospecting may look like hazing or similar to fraternity pledging, and that's probably how it was for past generations, but as I progressed in club life and through leadership, I saw prospecting as a way to teach potential members the club's history and protocol. It is how they learn the rules and see firsthand the level of commitment it takes to be in a club and gives both the club and the prospect the chance to see if they are able to find a balance between club life and personal life. Over the years, I've heard people outside club life say things like, "I would never be someone's bitch," and I always took offense at that. I would never want in my chapter or club anyone who is willing to be a "bitch." Prospecting is not to make anyone a servant; it is to teach them the club's pecking order and structure. It is to bring humility to all members and potential members and test their limits to see how a potential member prioritizes club life. Contrary to popular belief, a prospect's job is not to break the law or do things other members wouldn't do. In fact, the Mongols have a rule that a member cannot ask a prospect to do something they would not do themselves. The Mongols have a constitution and bylaws, and part of prospecting is getting to know those inside and out. One of the commandments the Mongols live by is that a Mongol shall not do anything that could get another Mongol arrested. This is the complete opposite of the idea promoted by some law enforcement agencies that prospects are used to commit crimes. The whole object of prospecting is to learn. Learn the club's program, history, and lifestyle, and make sure they are a good fit for you. Any task a prospect is asked to complete should be with the purpose of learning a lesson. If the prospect cannot learn from it, there is no point in asking the prospect to do it. At least that was always my perspective on prospecting, and why I never agreed with the old-school hazing some tried to do. The purpose of prospecting for the Outsiders MC was to learn its history and protocol and get to know each member. They did it right.

I wanted to impress the Outsiders and show them I was an asset to the club. I was pretty new to riding, and brand new at club life, but what I did have experience in was violence, and I looked for any opportunity that I could to show them how capable of violence I was. My first opportunity came when I was still a hang around. Fishnets, Lil Zac, and I were riding with a few of the Outsiders, hitting some local bars. Shortly after ordering our first drink some twenty-something-year-old kid walked up to an Outsider and said, "Do you think you're tough just because you ride a Harley?" I'm not sure what was said in return, but whatever it was set it off, and they stood toe-to-toe next to the video poker machines exchanging punches. I was excited. This was my chance. I looked for Fishnets, but he had just stepped into the restroom. I ran straight at the kid who started the fight and hit him with all I could in the side of his face, but before I could see his reaction, I was lifted off the ground and thrown across the room. All I could see were my feet and the bar ceiling. In my haste, I neglected to notice that I ran right past two of his friends, so when I hit him, they both grabbed me from behind, picked me up, and chucked me right across the room, where a table broke my fall. Fishnets had heard the commotion, but by the time he was able to zip up his leather pants, the action was over. This had been my chance and I missed it. When we got back to the clubhouse, the story was being shared, and for the remainder of the night I was called Chuck, since I was thrown across the bar. Not exactly the image I was working for.

Although I never took that bus ticket to Sacramento, vengeance for my brother never left my mind. It was about a year after the incident with DMS and my brother's assault. He was healed up and we were both spending a lot of time riding with the Outsiders. Due to his injuries, Rose City allowed him to step away without being jumped out. We had learned that a popular skinhead band, The Templars, were playing one West Coast show, and it would take place in Seattle. There was a strong chance that members of Most Hated and others involved in the attack on my brother would be attending this show, and we thought it might be our chance at revenge.

We had a pretty solid plan. We drove up during the day and attended a party at the Outsiders clubhouse in Tacoma. Jeremy, Lil Zac, and I left our wallets and cell phones at the clubhouse and drove in a borrowed car to the concert venue. We found a place to park where we could watch. Lil Zac went inside to see who was there because he was pretty good at blending in in a crowd. When he confirmed some of the guys we were looking for were there, we pulled on our masks and gloves, readied our weapons, and were just about to step out of the car when the entire block lit up with lights and sirens. There were cops and federal agents everywhere. They stormed the venue and had everyone outside up against the wall. We were far enough away that we had not been seen, so we watched as they handcuffed and loaded members of another gang, FSU (Friends Stand United), into a police bus. Apparently, FSU had been under investigation, and we hadn't been the only ones watching the venue–the FBI had a surveillance team there as well. Had we gotten out of the car any sooner, or had they waited a few more minutes before raiding, I would be telling this story from behind a prison wall. We hardly spoke the whole way back to the clubhouse. It was all sinking in how close we just were to prison. Everything could have gone very bad. When we got back to the clubhouse, no one asked how it went or even what we had been up to, and we just went back to partying, a little more grateful for our freedom than we had been earlier in the day.

We made it pretty clear after that that no DMS bands were welcome in Portland, and for over ten years, none of them came. Shortly after joining the Mongols, I got a call from a brother, The Rev, from Harbor chapter. I hadn't met Rev in person yet, but he was a veteran member in a very well-respected chapter of the Nation, and I had been in about two months when he called. He called to let me know that he and other members of the Harbor chapter were close with some of the guys from DMS, and he wanted to make it known that, as a rule, when you join the Mongols, you drop any old beefs. No member is to use the backup of the club against previous enemies–that would be using the patch for personal gain and could get you kicked out. At first, I was bummed about the phone call, but I also understood. For years, every time I would see Rev, we would talk about it, and we got pretty close over the whole thing. Other than once chasing a DMS member wearing their gang's colors like a motorcycle vest out of a concert in Pomona, I never threatened them or used the club's name in my favor. However, I can promise you it wouldn't have gone well had they ever tried to show up to an event.

The Drop Kick Murphy's singer was an ex-member of DMS, but he was no longer in, and they continued to play in Portland. I had met them many years earlier when I was on the run for beating up Matt Adamson, and later ran into them and had a bit of a misunderstanding that led to some of them getting punched in the face at one of their concerts in Portland. I became close with Ken, their bass player. He helped my band tour with Brain Failure, a band he was managing, shortly before we broke up. In fact, that was The Escaped's final tour. And we would stay in touch from time to time. Any time they played in Oregon, he would get me in and often with a large guest list. However, since my friends were either skinheads or Mongols, we were never very good guests. The last time was at the Roseland Theater in Portland in early 2008. Ken got something like eight or so of us in on the guest list. We were sitting upstairs in the bar section, and as Drop Kick hit the stage, this drunken guy behind us kept stomping his feet and spilling his beer on us. He was warned to knock it off, but he didn't heed the advice of his friends and kept it up, and it wasn't long before one of the Mongols punched him right in the face. He had friends with a him, and right away, we were in an all-out brawl on the balcony. One of the bigger Mongols grabbed the guy, picked him up, and threw him, and the whole fight paused as we watched the body fly through the air. I was convinced he was going over, but thankfully, he didn't make it past the railing. Once the bouncers came in and broke it up, we were escorted, very politely I might add, out of the venue. For some reason, they took us through backstage on our way out. The fight had stopped the concert, and as we were being shown out, I could see the disappointment in Ken's eyes.

I haven't asked for guest list spots or spoken to Ken since then. But last year, I took Ashley to see them in St. Louis, and their singer, my friend Al, got me on the guest list, but this time it was just plus one. They weren't going to let me bring an army in anymore.

Around the same time, I also met another popular band that I was into back then called Flogging Molly. We were spending a lot of time at a popular nightclub in downtown Portland. One trip home from Reno, our flight was delayed, and they gave us some drink vouchers. Once we got on the plane, they gave us some more. By the time we got to Portland, I was pretty lit, and we ended up going to our favorite downtown bar. Once inside, I got back to drinking, and toward the end of the night, a skinhead walked past me. He looked somewhat familiar, but I couldn't place him. And being a little buzzed up and being a hometown skinhead, I went up and asked him where he was from, half expecting to punch him. But he answered back that he was in town on tour and was in a band. When I said, "Oh yeah? What band?" he replied with "Flogging Molly," and we started shooting the shit. We told him we were fans and exchanged numbers so we could get on the guest list the next night at their show.

The following day, they were doing a record signing at a Portland record store and about six to eight Mongols rode to it and hung with them for a while and then rode to the show. The concert was fun and relatively uneventful, but after the show, we decided we were going to go back to the bar we had been spending a lot of our time at. We parked out front of the bar and walked across the street to a convenience store. I had noticed on our ride through downtown that we were gathering some police attention, but I didn't think much of it. But when we walked outside the store, we were quickly surrounded. But this wasn't an arrest. They rolled up on us like a rival gang. They quickly circled us, hands on their weapons, and asked what we were doing wearing our patches in their side of town. They were trying to provoke us, and for a short time, most of the group was provoked. I was standing in the middle, trying to cool down the scene, while this Portland cop asked, "What makes you think you can wear your patches down here?" Verbal assaults were going back and forth, and I seriously thought we were about to fight Portland gang cops. Thankfully, they parted and we passed. However, they followed us into the bar and went straight to the manager. That was our last night in that bar and following that almost all bars in downtown Portland adopted a new policy that no motorcycle club patches were allowed inside the bars.

My second chance to impress the Outsiders came when I was a prospect. Again, we were at a bar, and this heavyset fella stared at me and stood in my way anytime I tried to move around the bar. Before I reacted, I wanted to know whether he was friends with the club, or perhaps another club's member testing me, so I asked Redeye who the guy was, and he said he had no idea. A while later, I was outside with a Tacoma member and was attempting to go back inside the bar to check on Redeye. The guy stood in my way again, and when I asked him to move, he said, "Make me!" So I did. I punched him hard in the mouth, and he fell into me and stumbled toward the sidewalk. I backed up as he lunged forward and caught him with an uppercut that put him on the ground. The Tacoma Outsider was standing next to me, and Redeye was rushing out to help. By the time Redeye got outside, the guy was on the ground snoring, and the Tacoma Outsider announced, "He was fucking with the prospect so I knocked him out." As a prospect, I could not challenge the word of a member, and he was a visitor, so it would not have gone in my favor. Not for lack of trying, but that meant that my second attempt failed as well. I would never get the chance to show the Outsiders that I could fight.

I wasn't about to put myself through being jumped out after already being allowed to leave and, in any case, the idea caused some trouble. A lot of the members were guys I had grown up with. I thought of them as friends and they saw me the same way. I was still working in the porn store, whose owner was a RCBB member.

And Portland is not that big a city–if you grew up there, you knew everyone else who grew up there. While I was prospecting, I found myself looking around the room at a party, and thinking, if it weren't for the motorcycle club, I'd have nothing in common with the other people in this room. I mean no disrespect in that–they were a different generation, and the things they'd experienced and the ideas they talked about were the things and ideas of the generation before mine. So the idea started to grow on me that it was time to move on. To leave Portland and, probably, to leave Oregon. At the time, the Outsiders were the only thing keeping me in Portland, and I was starting to realize I was not the best fit for this club.

Popular opinion is that 99 percent of motorcycle club members are law-abiding citizens. At least, that's what the American Motorcycle Association said after a 1947 riot in Hollister, California, though anyone I've ever met who knew anything about the so-called Hollister Riot said the press had made a big fuss out of not very much. That left 1 percent, and members of those clubs were called one-percenters. One percenters belonged to motorcycle clubs like Hell's Angels, Outlaws, Bandidos, Gypsy Jokers, and Pagans and wore a patch to identify themselves. Or that's the widely accepted definition of one-percenters. My definition is much simpler. To me a 1 percenter is a member of one of the major, national, motorcycle clubs, often referred to as dominant or dominant clubs. On this basis, the Hell's Angels, Outlaws, Bandidos, Pagans, and Mongols all qualified and, in recent years, the Vagos also joined their ranks. The Outsiders started wearing a 1 percenter patch around 2017 or 2018, but I did not include them on my list as they are not a national club and are only in two states.

The Gypsy Jokers were the dominant club in Oregon, and they decided, in effect, what clubs could be formed. We knew something about the Gypsy Jokers because our biological father had hung out with them and, in fact, done time with them. (Within the last year or so, the president of the Portland chapter was sentenced to life imprisonment for murder.) I didn't feel ready to jump that deep into a world I otherwise knew very little about. The club I joined instead was the Outsiders. They'd been in Portland since the 1960s and they weren't yet 1 percenters, though that would come later.

My sponsor while I was prospecting with the Outsiders went by the name of Redeye. Kristin and I were still in an on-and-off relationship, though more off than on. Redeye worked in the same Harley dealership as Kristin and Jeremy and I met him when we bought our first bikes. Nothing came of that at the time because no self-respecting motorcycle club member in Oregon was going to hang out with someone who rides a Sportster, though clubs in some states saw it differently. You couldn't leave a Sportster in front of the Outsiders' clubhouse, and you couldn't give even the appearance of riding with a member (let alone in the pack) when that was all the bike you had. But then we traded up, our new bikes were acceptable, and Redeye started inviting us to hang out more.

Prospecting is damn hard work, and even someone as committed as I was can struggle—with sheer tiredness, if nothing else. I worked seven to three so that I'd have time to get to the clubhouse and do all the things I was expected to do—keep the place clean, keep the bar stocked, tend bar. Then I'd ride with the members. On the rare occasions they weren't going out that night, I'd go home, but you couldn't leave until a member cut you loose. I had very little home life and I was tired all the time. As an Italian family, Easter was a big time for us and I needed to get to Salem, an hour away. I explained that to the president who said, "It'll be fine. We'll cut you loose in time." And they did, about six in the morning, so I was able to go home, change, and go straight into a big family Easter without a moment of sleep. I was completely drug-free at that time; maybe if I hadn't been, I'd have managed the sleeplessness better. Haircut, the Outsiders president, had been in the club a long time, but he was younger than most of the established members, and he found out that I wasn't into drugs. He told me that if he ever found out that the club had got me into taking drugs, he wouldn't vote for me to be a full patch member. And if the president doesn't vote for you, you don't get in. For me, that was a great insight into what club membership could be, and what great leadership meant.

While all this was going on, I got a call from a member of the Rose City Bovver Boys. "Where are you? We are going to jump you out. Tell me where you're at."

I said, "I'm right here outside the Outsiders clubhouse. You're welcome to come down and talk to me here." I didn't hear from them again, and I never was jumped out. We reconnected years later, but I don't remember that time with any pleasure.

Put all those things together and I was ready for a move. Then I got a call from a cousin who lived in Carson City, Nevada. Her husband worked for a gas company that was updating gas meters and she thought he could get me a job there. And, if that didn't work out right away, he had a friend who was an electrician, and he could get me taken on there. So now I started to think not only about wanting a move but also about where my life was going to take me. Even if I'd stayed in RCBB, managing an adult video store is not a lifetime location. Working for a gas company or an electrician could just be the beginning of some kind of career.

The Outsiders were really cool about my leaving. Because I was going out of state and because I was doing it for work, they hung up my vest and told me I could be an inactive prospect; if I came back, the time I'd already spent prospecting would count in my favor. They also gave me introductions to motorcycle clubs in Nevada. So I mailed a box of clothes to my cousin's address and rode my bike to Carson City. Jeremy and Lil Zac rode the first half of the journey with me, and we stayed the night in a motel on the Oregon/Nevada border. Then in the morning, they peeled off and I rode the rest of the way on my own.

I started out working as an electrician's apprentice and then, when a job opened up at the gas company, I moved across to that.

I still, though, saw motorcycling as the center of my life, and I was itching for a ride. I had met a member of Boozefighters motorcycle club and they were going up to Reno for a Confederation of Clubs meeting that happened every couple months. He invited me to ride with them and I saw that as a chance to meet some of the local clubs. When we got there, every club in northern Nevada was present. I used to wear a denim vest over a leather jacket. As it turned out, that was what the Vagos wore, which made me feel a little nervous, but the Vagos just ignored me.

When the meeting was over, the Boozefighters took me inside and introduced me to their club. They also introduced me to the Hells Angels, which was the first time I'd ever met a Hells Angel. When the Boozefighters left, they gave me directions to a bar where they said they'd be hanging out. And I got lost trying to find the bar. And it was worse than that because I found my way to a bar where I thought the Boozefighters might be, but in fact, it was filled with Vagos. I wasn't going to just turn around and drive away–I didn't want to look like a pussy–so I went into the bar, aware that people were looking at me and talking about me. Who the hell was I, and what the hell did I think I was doing walking uninvited into a Vagos bar dressed like one of them? I didn't drink at that time, but I thought a weapon might be useful, and so I bought a bottle of beer.

When this guy walked up to me, I was braced for anything, but he introduced himself as Awful Al, one of the presidents of the Vagos. We ended up talking for about two hours. I told him about my history and that I had prospected for the Outsiders in Portland and that I was starting a new job the next day as an electrician's apprentice. When we parted, he gave me his Vagos courtesy card with his phone number, and I gave him mine.

Midday the next day, I stopped work to get something to eat and checked my phone. There was a message from Awful Al saying he hoped my first day was going well, and if there was anything I needed, I should call.

That had a hell of an impact on me. I was here in Nevada, on my own, and somebody was taking the time to make sure I was okay. And not any somebody—we're talking about a president of a highly respected motorcycle club. The result was simple: I started hanging out with Al, riding with him, having dinner with him, to the point where I wasn't turning up for work, and I moved over to work for the Carson City Harley dealership. But that didn't work out because selling motorcycles isn't something you can combine with membership of a club. You make your money at weekends, but that's also when club rides take place.

The first time I saw all of the Vagos together was on a run to Las Vegas, and what I realized was that it was different from the Outsiders. There were a lot of younger guys, a lot of Hispanics, a lot of guys who were into punk rock instead of classic rock, a lot of guys like me. Being a Vago started to feel like home. By then, Jeremy had started prospecting for the Outsiders, but I kept telling him how good it felt, and he would come down from Portland to ride with us for the weekend. In the end, he left the Outsiders and moved to Carson City, we got a place together, and we both joined the Vagos at the same time. Because we had been prospects for the Outsiders and because we were starting a new Bordertown chapter of the Vagos as an offshoot from the Reno chapter, we both got our patches straight away at a hotel in Nevada. We were there as hang arounds but rode home as full patched members. When Awful Al handed us our patches, he told us we had an hour to sew them on to our denim vests, and then we were expected to link back up and go out with the chapter. We were given a needle and a spool of thread. I wasn't much into sewing and was rushing to get my patch sewn on when I realized I had sewn my vest and patch to the ironing board I was using to sew on. It was a reminder of when I was given my prospect patches for the Outsiders and, in my haste, sewed part of my top rocker to the club's pool table. Another reputation that took a while to live down.

It wasn't long after that that I got my nickname. We had ridden to a national run in Hollister, California. It was my first big Vago run, and although I was excited, the excitement waned quickly when we got to the campground. It was 114 degrees, and the campground was just one wide open field with no shade or water in sight. It had been a long day, and Al had given me permission to go back to the campground and rest for a bit. When he and the chapter got back to the campsite, he found me sitting in one of the few chairs eating lunch. He looked at me and said, "Where did you get that chair?" and I said, "Joe said I could use it." "Where did you get food?" "Glenn made it." "Is that a new shirt?" "Yeah, Berry got it for me." "Didn't I give you that hat?" "Sure did, Boss." Then Al chuckled and said, "Damn, you are a mooch," and that was it. He had me walk around from campsite to campsite and introduce myself and whenever I said, "Mooch, Bordertown chapter," someone would reply with, "Mooch, huh? Well what can I get ya? Need a burger or a beer or somethin'?" And just like that, I never went hungry again.

The next big run was to the National Harley Drags in Las Vegas. The Vagos all met up outside town and then rode in one big pack to the drag strip. This was the biggest pack I had ever ridden in up to then and I was buzzing from it. As we pulled into the parking lot, a Hells Angel pulled up next to us on what I assume was a built Road Glide and rode a wheelie past our entire pack. In the Outlaw club world, it is considered disrespectful to pass another club, and this was just the start of what became an eventful day. There were a lot of other major clubs at this event and other than the chatter of the Angels having an issue, everything was going pretty well. As the event wound down and we walked toward our bikes that quickly changed. For some reason unknown to me, the Vagos left in a few groups instead of all together. Our chapter was in the smaller group that was leaving last. Apparently as we left the venue, the Hells Angels had noticed a Vago wearing an Arizona rocker. The Vagos opening in Arizona had been the source of tension with the

Hells Angels all day, but I guess actually seeing it set them off. A few angry Angels walked into the middle of the group of Vagos and grabbed the Arizona member and asked who was in charge. The Vagos, thinking they had the advantage due to having the Angels outnumbered, surrounded the Angels. I had been watching the Angels throughout the day and knew there were a lot more of them there than their whereabouts, so I backed out of the group and tried to get behind the large circle to make sure we didn't get surrounded. I looked over next to me and saw a minivan parked next to our bikes, and at least one of the people in it was holding a rifle. Jeremy and I tried to get behind the perimeter so that no one could sneak up on the group, and as we did, we noticed a group of Hells Angels prospects with a saddlebag open, and they were handing pistols to the rest of the prospects. Due to the drag strip having security and a lot of law enforcement, the Vagos had told its members not to bring firearms, so as well as being surrounded, we were also outgunned. Jeremy and I began to tell some of the Vagos near us what was going on, and CK, a member from our chapter, said, "If they start shooting, we charge them." That was his plan. Jeremy and I were not stoked on the idea, but we also weren't going to leave our brothers behind. Just as things seemed like they were about to kick off, a police helicopter hovered overhead, and an officer with a bullhorn demanded that the crowd disperse. Quickly, a large presence of LVPD on horseback appeared and were forcing everyone to split up. We got on our bikes and rode out, and the whole way home all I could think about was how impressed I was with the Hells Angels tactics. I vowed never to allow our arrogance to put us in a position like that again.

Being young and immature, I still had ideas going into the Vagos about showing my ability to fight. Shortly after joining, our chapter was at a small bar out in the desert. The kind of bar that has just as many ATVs as pickup trucks parked out front. We were sitting around having some drinks when we heard a pack of bikes pull up, and we saw these guys walk in wearing denim vests, and, although I could see they were wearing patches, I could not see what they said. I got up and walked over to the food line as the group made their way in. As they walked by other members of the Vagos, they locked eyes and pushed their way through. By the time they got to me, everyone had already had enough, and when their leader attempted to push me, I hit him right in the face. His forehead immediately split open and the whole bar turned into a brawl. At one point the bartender came out from behind the bar and was hitting me with a broomstick, trying to break it up. I was pushed out the front door and the other club was pushed out the back. I ran around back and the guy I had hit was leaning up against a picnic table, looking dazed and disheveled. I was just about to set in on him again when Awful Al grabbed me and ordered me to stand down. I was standing there, catching my breath, when the beaten club turned around and walked toward their bikes. And that is when I saw their patch. It read "Over the Hill Club." It was a senior citizens' club. I earned a reputation with the chapter that day, but it definitely wasn't the one I was going for.

During my time in the skinhead scene, I had learned a lot about street combat, but the level of violence in the club world was much more serious. It was much less about simple fist fights and things often progressed to stabbings and shootings, so security was much more important. Another thing I still hadn't learned was the process of sitting down with another club. Often clubs would sit down with each other to hammer out any potential issues before they escalated to violence. My first experience with this was as a Vago, and it was with the Hells Angels. The Hells Angels are one of those clubs everyone knows about, even if they know nothing else about the biker world. They've been in the mainstream media for years, often for serious crimes, and it is ingrained in many of us that they are the "real deal." Going from a small club in Oregon to a club that was having issues with the Hells Angels was a pretty big culture shock. The Vagos and Hells Angels weren't getting into it yet, but when I joined, tensions were high and things were only going to get worse.

Years before my time, the Vagos had shut down a club in Reno called The Renegades. The way it was told to me was that there was an agreement with the Hells Angels and there would never again be Renegades in the Reno area. Shortly after I had joined the Vagos, the Renegades started back up. This made for popular discussion within the club and was my first introduction to things getting dangerous in club life. Back in Oregon, at least in the Valley, there were only four major clubs: The Gypsy Jokers, Brother Speed, The Outsiders, and The Free Souls. For the most part, they got along. They often went to each other's parties and would be seen hanging together at local bars. So, living in an area where clubs had enemies was new to me. I was used to the concept, which was much like RCBB fighting with Volksfront, but the level of violence was much greater. In Reno, the next Confederation of Clubs meeting was coming up and word was the Renegades were going to be there. There were a lot of meetings within the chapter and with other Vagos chapters in the area about what could happen at this meeting. We had planned to get there two hours early so we could set up surveillance and control the exits and entrances to the parking lot, but when we got there, we found out the Hells Angels had gotten their well before us. Not only did they have members posted all around the building and parking lot, but they had cars posted up that could block the entrance and exit to the building if needed. Although it wasn't in our favor, I was very impressed, and it was obvious why they were well-known and such a premier club. The Hells Angels have fought many wars in their time, and they have clearly adapted to being a warring club. In fact, a lot of what I learned that night I took with me for when I was doing sit-downs with other clubs in years to come. They had plainclothes members as well as patched members in various parts inside and outside the building. We were communicating with Awful Al inside via cell phone and then with the others spread out around the parking lot via walkie-talkie. As the sun set and things started to get dark, tensions rose. The Renegades were there and the Hells Angels were protecting them. At one point, things came very close to getting bad, perhaps a story for another time, but thankfully the event ended without any bloodshed, and we all went home for the night.

However, things with the Hells Angels were only going to get worse in coming months. Between the issue with the Vagos starting new chapters in Arizona and the Renegades starting back up in Reno, things were getting very tense. There had been some more close calls after both the Harley Drags and the COC meeting, but so far nothing had escalated to violence. That was about to change. The Vagos had just started a new chapter in Redding, California, historically well-known to be a strictly Hells Angels area. That was bad enough, but these new members came from a club with a close relationship with the Angels and had a recent falling out, so not only was it a slap in the face, but it was also personal. Shortly after their chapter started, the Redding Vagos were attacked at their clubhouse, and soon we were getting calls to head over the mountain to back them up. It was only about two and a half hours from our chapter so we were often the chapter to get the call.

Cherokee, a friend of mine from way back, was visiting for the first time, and I'd really been looking forward to the weekend with her, but when you get a call like that, you go. We piled into a car and drove to Redding, where we met not only Redding Vagos but also some from Sacramento. The leadership told us we needed to attack the Jus Brothers, a Hells Angels support club. I didn't see this as a genius idea; the Jus Brothers clubhouse was fortified, it had security cameras, and there would be weapons in there. But that was the order from the leadership, so that's what we had to do. No one was wearing anything Vago related—no colors, no patches—but when we arrived, there was no one there. I don't mean temporarily; they'd moved. They had a different clubhouse. So now, as well as questioning the leadership's decisions, I found myself wondering about their intelligence gathering. Still, we were there, we'd been given a mission, so we started hitting bars, trying to find some of their guys.

Across the road from one bar that had been a Jus Brothers hangout, we saw a guy watching us from a mobile home across the road. After a few minutes, he walked over to see what all these guys were doing at his bar. He found out pretty soon what was going on and he was surrounded by Vagos. In my experience, when someone on his own is surrounded like that, he's going to run and he's probably going to run home, so I moved away from the group and put myself between the bar and the mobile home. He was looking backward and forwards between this menacing crowd around him and the skinny kid blocking his way to his house, so he ran straight at me, and when I hit him, he changed direction and ran into a Circle K. Some of the Vagos followed him in there, took his patch, and beat him up. Then we headed back home, where Cherokee was still waiting for me, having spent twenty-four hours on her own.

Awful Al's chapter was holding a party that we went to. Across the road was the Bunny Ranch, a well-known whorehouse where we liked to hang out from time to time, and that turned out to be the only really wild Vago party I was ever part of. It was an eye-opener for Cherokee, who'd never hung with bikers before.

That was pretty well in the end of our time around the trouble between Vagos and Hells Angels in California because Jeremy and I knew it was time to go back home. We went out to dinner and then to a bar. It turned out there was a girl working in that bar who'd had a thing for Jeremy for a long time but never spoken to him. That changed that night and, when she realized he was about to leave, they talked for a long time and exchanged phone numbers. When she finished work, we went to another bar where there was a big group of Vagos, and some guy we didn't know said something flattering to the Hells Angels and unflattering to us, and I hit him. It was only after I'd hit him that I realized, *This is a big dude.* After taking my punch, he said, "That all you got?" If I'd had any sense, I'd have shaken his hand and bought another beer, but I was young and arrogant. "Okay," I said, "let's go!"

"Oh, you're just being brave because you got all your friends here."

"I'm gonna leave my friends in here. Let's you and me step outside."

So we did. It went all right at first, but then he picked me up and threw me on the ground, and he was just wailing on me. I'm thinking, *Hey, my brother's inside, any minute now he is gonna come out and get this guy off me*. What I didn't understand was that Jeremy had fallen in love with this chick, and he was too busy romancing her to wonder where his brother was. Eventually, the others didn't realize I was outside so they came out to see what was going on, and then they shouted to tell Jeremy I was being beaten up. Jeremy came racing out, assumed I was winning and started to kick the guy on the bottom, which was me. Then the guy realized he was outnumbered and he took off. We chased after him, but law enforcement intervened.

I had to spend an extra three days in Carson City because of a combination of alcohol poisoning and being beat up, and Jeremy stayed with me. The result of that was that he spent more time with Megan and they are now happily married.

Monkey Joe had been an original member of the Rose City Bovver Boys. He had stepped out before I was jumped in, but I had always heard stories of him and everyone seemed to look up to him. He was the smoothest dressed member and carried himself with class, or so it appeared. After moving back to Oregon, I reconnected with Joe via social media and was happy to learn he too was riding Harleys. We started talking often and eventually started hanging out and riding often. Often, when I had to ride Southern Oregon for club meetings or events, Joe would ride with me. We were spending a lot of time together, and because of our shared background, I really trusted the man. Joe was still a hang around at the time, and we were all meeting up in Southern Oregon, getting ready to ride to Street Vibrations in Reno for a big Vago national run. Kristin wanted to work things out, so she came down a day before we left, and she stayed with me. Joe and another hang around from Portland had a hotel room together. I had to work the day we were getting ready to leave, and Joe and James were planning on going for a ride and checking out all of the covered bridges in Oregon. Not being the possessive or controlling type, and fully trusting Joe, I suggested he take Kristin with them on the ride. It wasn't even that Kristin and I were serious at this time, but we had a long history by now and obviously were more than just friends. Both Rose City and the Vagos had rules around messing with another member's girlfriend without permission. With both groups, the offense usually resulted in expulsion.

The run was a good time and nothing too wild happened. As it was wrapping up, we were getting ready to head back to Oregon and Joe and James were going to continue on to Las Vegas. Joe asked Kristin if she wanted to go to Vegas with them. Obviously, it struck me as odd, but I had too much trust in Joe to think it was anything more than friends. Kristen didn't go, and we parted ways with Joe and James.

It was brought to my attention a few days later, while Kristin was still staying with me, that she and Joe had been texting a lot and making plans to see each other when he got back to Oregon. I was pretty upset due to the violation of trust, and when Joe and James came through town on their way home, I visited them at their hotel. I took Magpie and Slider from the Vagos with me to keep everyone calm. James denied knowing about it, and Joe swore it was only in friendship and he had no ill intentions. I explained my history with Kristin and how it would hurt me if someone I considered a friend affected my relationship; he said he understood and that he would respect my wishes. We ended the conversation with a handshake and hug and we left. Magpie and I spoke on the way back and neither of us felt good about the conversation. We had both felt Joe wasn't being honest. Joe was supposed to start prospecting soon, and we were having doubts about his honesty and loyalty.

A few days later, while Magpie and I were at work laying tile, we got a call from Joe saying that he didn't think he was ready to start prospecting. The Vagos had a rule (back then, I doubt it is still a rule today), that if you failed as a prospect, you had to give the club your motorcycle, and he didn't want to risk losing his bike. He named health issues and financial troubles as to why he had to take a step back. Once we were both off the phone, we knew it had to do with Kristin. Just days before the call, she had left to go back home with her mom, or so she told me. As it turned out, she moved in with Joe. I didn't know this quite yet and was still talking to Joe as a friend. In fact, I'd even invited him to come to Daytona with me to meet the Mongols. Joe had told me in the past he'd been a hang around with the Hells Angels when he lived in San Francisco, but he'd had to get out of the state after sleeping with a high-ranking member's girlfriend. That should have been a warning sign. I later learned that he'd had a similar reason for leaving Rose City. Once I found all of this out, I was very upset. I felt betrayed. I had ignored a lot of signs and continued to be friends with someone who lied and was disloyal to me. And I wanted to make it right.

Once a prospect or member of a club leaves the club, they are usually required to return all club items such as patches, tee shirts, jewelry etc. Although Joe never made it to the prospect phase, I decided I didn't want him representing the club I was in anymore so I told him he needed to box up all of his support shirts and bring them to me. He was apprehensive so I suggested to bring them to James's house. James lived with Fishnets at the time. Jeremy picked me up and we drove over to Fishnets to wait for Joe to arrive. We sat on the front porch, telling Fishnets what had happened, and while we were doing that, I unrolled some painter's plastic and started to put it down on the porch. When Fishnets asked what I was doing, I replied very matter of fact, "When Joe walks up here with his shirts, I'm going to shoot him." Fishnets was not happy and said, "At my house?" Jeremy didn't take it too seriously, and I told Fishnets that

I only intended to shoot him in the knee, not to kill him. Jeremy laughed and said, "Oh yeah? With what gun?" and I reached into my waistband and showed Jeremy a small pistol I had swiped from his room before we left. Now he was pissed off too. As it turned out, there was no need to get upset. Joe never showed up. He called James and asked him to meet him at Portland Airport to pick up the box, literally the safest place he could meet.

That was the end of my long and tumultuous relationship with Kristin. I didn't see Joe or speak to him in quite some time after that either. Joe ended up joining the Free Souls and I ended up leaving the Vagos and joining the Mongols. Another old-school member of Rose City, Smiley, was getting into Harleys and started spending a lot of time with Joe. Smiley also ended up joining the Free Souls. It bummed me out that guys from my past, from the same gang as me, joined another club, but it also made sense. I didn't leave Rose City on the best of terms, plus who in their right mind would want to join a club that was close to being at war with every other club in the state? So, I don't blame him.

Unfortunately, Joe and Smiley got into drugs together and Smiley ended up dead from an overdose. Smiley was one of the most respected Bovver Boys, a founder and original member, and it hit us all really hard. Due to our past connection, the Free Souls were gracious enough to allow us to ride to Smiley's funeral and be there for the services. This was the first time I had seen Monkey Joe since the day in that hotel room. It wasn't the time nor the place and to be honest, I didn't care about it anymore. His thing with Kristin didn't work out, and she ended up marrying another man. I'm sure it wasn't a great relationship experience for him, yet I thought it was what he deserved. I smiled and said hello to him and asked how he was going. He was cordial but short and moved on quickly. I turned to Jeremy and said, "What's his problem?" and Jeremy replied, "I'd assume he knows you were going to shoot him." We both laughed and went on to say good-bye to our old friend.

I was a Vago for about two years. When I first moved to Carson City, my cousin's husband had said, "Hey, there's a Mongol who goes to our church." I'd heard of the Mongol motorcycle club, but I'd never met a member. The man in question was Coconut Dan, and my cousin and her husband didn't know him very well so, although I thought it would be good to meet him, it didn't happen at that time. Then one night we were at The Bonanza in Reno and a bunch of Mongols visited. The meeting ended up going fine, but it was our first introduction to the Mongols, and we saw firsthand the air of intimidation that went with them. At first, it was just an old man and a young guy who came by car and I didn't think much of them, but it turned out they were reconnoitering for about thirty Mongols on bikes who were waiting some distance away. Then they made a phone call and the thirty turned up at The Bonanza. Coconut Dan and their local president, Roy, came up to my president and asked if the twins were there. By twins, they meant me and Jeremy.

Jeremy and I had been thinking about moving back to Oregon, and, when I was offered a job there, we decided to go. The job was with a company owned by a Vago so I knew I'd always be able to get time off to ride with the Vagos. I'd gotten to know Coconut Dan a little since that meeting in Reno; we never got close, but we'd see each other around from time to time and talk, so I looked him up and told him I was going back to Oregon. He said he didn't think there were any Mongols up there, but he gave me his Mongols courtesy card with his number on it and said if I ever needed anything, I should call him. That impressed me, so when I did decide I wanted to be a Mongol, he was the first person I called. What I didn't know at that time was that he was a paid informant for both the DEA and the ATF (though never actually an agent).

When we got back to Oregon, we joined one of the two Vagos chapters there. We stayed in the Vagos for another year or so, but something began to bother me about it. One of the things I really liked about the Outsiders was that they had a rule that said there was nothing that could happen between two brothers (by which they meant two members), that the brothers couldn't settle by sitting down and talking about it. And that was also a Vago rule. Members were not allowed to fight members. In theory. But not always in practice. A Vago I knew called Wild Bill had been down in Mexico at a party thrown by a number of Vago chapters and fights had broken out between some of them. Then, on his way home, he was shot off his bike and killed. Vagos would never say it was Vagos who killed him, but that was my suspicion, and not only mine. And it turned out that a number of Vago chapters had beefs with each other, and some of the ways they were settling them were no better than I'd seen at the time I had the band and we got on the wrong side of DMS. I thought about it long and hard, and I knew I wasn't cool with the way things were developing. This was not what I'd signed up for.

I was about to become a Mongol.

CHAPTER FIVE

A T THE END OF the last chapter, I said I was about to become a Mongol. That's easy to say; the reality is a bit more complicated. Most people in America aren't bikers and, of those who are, only a very small number are 1 percenters (the clue is in the name). So, what most Americans know about motorcycling clubs is what they read in the press or see in television news bulletins. The biker life the press and TV describe often has very little to do with the life bikers actually lead. Here's an introduction to the world of the 1 percenter.

Territory is extremely important. You can't just go to a new area and set up a new club, or a new chapter of an existing club, without the permission of the dominant club in that area. Very bloody battles have been fought over long periods to enforce that rule. For example, a lot of people died on both sides before the Gypsy Jokers and the Hells Angels came to an agreement: the Jokers would rule in Oregon and stay out of California while the Angels would be number one in California but stay out of Oregon. And the Mongols were about to challenge the Jokers' Oregon dominance, just as they had tested the Hells Angels' dominance in California decades earlier. There were Mongols in Nevada, as we've already seen, and they planned to set up chapters in Oregon.

I called Coconut Dan, not knowing that he was a paid informant for the ATF, and I told him I'd read on the Mongols' website that they were thinking of setting up in Oregon and, if there was anything Jeremy and I could do, just to let us know. I then got a call from

Lars, president of the Mongols' World chapter, which had the job of setting up new chapters in new areas. He realized pretty fast that I was interested in more than just helping the Mongols out, and he invited me out to Daytona Beach in Florida where there was about to be a bike fest. So I flew on my own to Florida in a Vagos T-shirt. Florida was an Outlaws state–the Outlaws had recently closed down a Vagos chapter that had just been set up in neighboring Georgia, and the Mongols had just set up in the state. I spent the weekend with Mongols, and we really hit it off.

I went with Lars to a meeting with the Outlaws in a strip club. This was the first time I had met any Outlaws. The bouncers effectively corralled us, frisking us, taking any weapons from us. (They said they'd keep them behind the bar and we'd get them back later.) I could tell from rings and stuff the bouncers were wearing that they were 1 percenters; in fact, they were all Outlaws in plain clothes. A bunch of Outlaws showed up and they went out the back to talk to Lars. The rest of us were kept inside; we couldn't go out, couldn't see what was happening to Lars, couldn't even go to the bathroom. Then Coconut Dan said he was going outside to check on Lars and he went, but he didn't come back. One of the Mongols said to me, "Hey, man, we don't know whether we're gonna get out of here, but you're not with us; you're welcome to leave." I just wasn't gonna do that. I was here with them and I was gonna stay. I was as concerned as they were. I texted my brother and told him I didn't know if I was gonna get out of this, but I stayed.

In fact, it ended peacefully, and the fact that I stayed with them made the difference to becoming a Mongol. They said, "You want to start a chapter? Start one. How many men you got?" And I was given the green light to start working on starting a Mongol chapter in Oregon. So I flew home and talked to the members of my Vagos chapter about patching over to the Mongols. Some wanted to stay in the Vagos, and others wanted to come with me. We did our interview with Lars and a very well-respected, longtime member of the Mongols in Carson City, and then Lars handed patches to me, Jeremy, and Lil T. Although Lil T lived in Carson City, he was joining the World chapter.

Doc was the Mongols' National president and he was on a major recruitment drive. He wanted to build a club strong enough and big enough to challenge the Hells Angels. During my first year in the club, I remember reading articles and seeing things on the news that reported that Doc was recruiting new members straight from the neighborhood gangs of Los Angeles. Because my love of motorcycles is what led me to join a motorcycle club, when I meet new members I often ask, "What kind of bike do you ride?" More than I would like to admit, during my first year or two in the club, I would sometimes get the answer, "I don't ride." I was unhappy about this, but too new in the club to question the leadership.

Going from the Outsiders to the Vagos was a common enough move. It often happened that guys joined smaller clubs, and then, as they learned more about club life, moved on to larger clubs. Going from Vagos to Mongols was less common. Clubs typically have agreements with other major clubs or rules that prevent people from going from one major club to another. The Vagos, although a bigger club, were still growing in 2007 but were not the national club they are today. Had I tried to leave the Vagos and join the Mongols in just about any other era, I wouldn't have been allowed to, but I came in during Doc's recruitment drive. When we decided to patch over some other Vagos from Oregon, Nevada, and shortly after, the Redding Vagos, it wasn't a smooth transition. While I was down in Carson City for my interview, the Vagos were attempting to break into my garage back home and steal my bike, but I had half expected that and had some old friends from the Cherry City Skins watching for them and they kept my bike safe. Nothing gets skinheads more excited than the chance for some violence and they were happy to help.

Within a few months of being a Mongol, Jeremy and I were both visited by FBI agents. I was staying at my mom's home at the time, and Jeremy was living in Portland with Megan. Legally, if law enforcement hears of a credible threat on someone's life, they have a duty to protect or warn that person. The FBI told us that they had an informant within the Vagos who had warned them that the Vagos had a "hit" on us both. Now, I didn't really believe things like that were real, especially back then, and I assumed it was just law enforcement trying to get us to ask for help or protection, but my mom took it very seriously. She was not happy. Either way, it was safe to say it was not a smooth transition.

We sat in Lil T's house in Carson City while his wife sewed on our patches. I was both anxious and excited. She handed them to us when they were done, and I put mine on and couldn't stop smiling. It was so crazy to think I was a Mongol now. I remember walking into the casino in Carson City with my patch on for the first time in public and the wave of adrenaline it gave me. Not only was it letting everyone in the casino know that I was a member of one of the most notorious motorcycle clubs in the world, but it also made me a target for the Hells Angels. I felt excited and nervous at the same time in a way that is hard to describe. My heart was racing.

We ended up going out to some bars with Lars and meeting up with the rest of World chapter. Two of the members there, Peligroso and Dozer, had been with me in Florida during my visit and our interaction with the Outlaws. It was great seeing them again, and we spent the night having some drinks and catching up. I could tell the vibe was shifting a bit toward the end of the night. I overheard Lars and some of the World chapter guys say, "Should we do it?" and my mind was racing. I instantly thought back to getting jumped into Rose City. "Could these guys really be talking about jumping me in?" I never did ask what the process was, I suppose. And then a few of the guys went out into the cold parking lot. It was November in northern Nevada, winter, and no one in their right mind would be hanging outside in this weather. I was mentally preparing for getting jumped when Lars told us to follow him outside. I thought, *Here we go.* I looked at Jeremy and couldn't tell whether he was thinking the same thing. Soon all of the Mongols had me, Jeremy, and Lil T surrounded, each of them holding a bottle of beer. I was getting ready to be hit with a beer bottle when someone shouted, "Who the fuck are we?" and the Mongols proceeded to chant the Mongols' fight song while covering us in beer. It was official. We were Mongols now; there was no turning back.

Lars and World chapter spent a lot of time in Carson City in the beginning so my first few months as a Mongol saw me going back and forth between Nevada and Oregon. One month after getting our patches, the World chapter hosted a Mongol national run at NV 50, the bar where just a year earlier I had partied with the Vagos and Cherokee. Mongols from all over California and the West Coast came to celebrate, and it was our first real introduction to the nation as a whole. It was powerful. These dudes carried themselves a lot different than the other clubs I had been around. Even when partying, they stayed serious. The vibe was heavy. There were some real killers in this room. It was here that I first met the Dago chapter. There weren't many white members when we joined, and Dago were all younger white guys at the time, so we instantly hit it off, and I spent most of the weekend with them. Dago Bull gave me my first gift as a member of the Mongols: a hat that read, "Fuck The Hells Angels." The night ended with the Mongols all doing the fight song in unison, and it was unlike anything I had ever seen or felt before. I commemorated both the weekend and my commitment to the Mongol Nation that weekend by tattooing Mongols MC across the back of my head as large as it would go. A picture of this tattoo was later used in an article by the *Oregonian* newspaper that announced the Mongols' presence in Oregon and became the most widely used photo in any article about the Mongols for many years.

As a Vago, I had been spending a good amount of time with the Free Souls in Eugene. I and a few other Vagos had been working in Eugene for a few months doing tile for the new Sacred Heart Hospital. Since I was staying there during the week for work, I would find time to ride around with the Free Souls when I could and attend some of their local events. I had developed a good relationship with them, and on my way home from Nevada, with new patches in hand, I knew the Free Souls were going to be upset. They had been very hospitable to me as a Vago, and I was returning that hospitality by starting the first chapter of the Oregon Mongols right here in Eugene, where their Mother chapter was located. I wanted to salvage as much of the relationship as I could, so on the drive home I called Doug, their president, and requested a sit-down with him. After seeing how bad meetings could go with other clubs, I was not going to leave anything to chance. The meeting was at a relatively busy bar/restaurant. I had some close friends go down several hours before the meeting and sit spread out around the bar to not be noticed and to see if they could spot any plainclothes Free Souls in or around the bar. I had two vehicles with members in the parking lot looking for other cars but also as back up if things didn't go well. And at the agreed time my brother and I walked into the bar in our Mongols patches and sat down with Doug. I felt bad. Doug had been good to us and we put him in a bad position. But if I wanted to make it as a Mongol, I needed to be professional and keep my feelings out of it. I told Doug we were starting a Mongols chapter in Eugene. I told him we were not asking for his permission, but out of courtesy, we were letting him know. I made it a point to let him know that we had zero issues with the Free Souls, and that unless they forced us to defend ourselves, they would have no problems with us. When I got up to leave, I made a circular motion with my index finder in the air, a sort of "round 'em up" gesture, and the dozen or so guys I had spaced out around the bar stood up and walked out with us once the lookout outside let us know our path was clear. We met up at a private residence afterwards to let the membership know how it went and to celebrate. The Mongols were officially in Oregon and no one was going to stop us. This was a speech I gave over a dozen times since then as I helped the Mongols expand all over the world.

CHAPTER SIX

ALTHOUGH I DIDN'T REALIZE it at the time, paid informants were involved pretty well all the way through my motorcycle club life. Instead of interrupting every chapter to mention what they were doing at that point, I'm devoting this whole chapter to the subject.

When I first started hanging out with motorcycle clubs, I was still pretty much a kid, naïve about the world and what really went on as opposed to what I'd read or seen on the screen. When it came to informants, I only knew what I had seen in movies or read in books. Because we were never breaking any major laws, it wasn't something I ever thought worth worrying about. I knew law enforcement kept an eye on motorcycle clubs, but I also knew that, other than defending each other or maybe having some personal use drugs on them, no one was really rising to the level of "organized crime." I knew frat boys who were committing more crimes than we were. But this is what I mean when I describe myself as naïve. I had read about undercover agents infiltrating different clubs over the years, but confidential informants was something I didn't know even existed. But they did and they do. They aren't cops–they are guys who have been arrested for breaking the law and, instead of doing their time, they choose to tell on others. And some of them are paid. We had no idea at the time, but there were two paid confidential informants in the Oregon chapters shortly after we started, and two other informants around the chapter. All four were paid to let local and federal law enforcement know what we were up to and to try to entrap us in crimes.

The first was known as Irish. Irish was an ex-Mongol from the Bay Area who had moved to Oregon and was trying really hard to hang out with the Vagos. Irish had somehow contacted a Vago named Quicky John. Quicky told us about him and suggested we meet up. There was something off about Irish from the very start. He was one of those guys who would start off a sentence with, "Hey, did you hear?" He made it sound like he was well connected to the club scene and knew a lot of the gossip and drama between clubs. Irish was texting and calling me often and telling me the Free Souls had a problem with me working in Eugene. I was a Vago at the time and there were no chapters that far north, so according to Irish, a lot of the clubs in the area were concerned that I was trying to start a Vago chapter in the Valley. What Irish didn't know was that I was very close to the Free Souls. When I talked to them about what he said, they told me he was also telling stories about the Outsiders.

I invited Irish for a drink at a bar near his home. I got there before him and I was with a few member of the Free Souls, but they were dressed in plainclothes with nothing signifying they were club members. When Irish got there, I told him they were friends of mine, and we all ordered drinks. As the night progressed, I asked Irish to tell me again what the Free Souls had told him. He told his story about how the Free Souls had told him they were going to come after me, and one of the guys at the table interrupted and said, "That didn't happen. And I know because we are the Free Souls." Right away, Irish started backtracking and saying he must have been mistaken; it was something he had heard from the Outsiders. I made a quick call and told Irish we were going to another bar to meet the Outsiders. He was visibly shaken and kept saying he needed to go home first. He was in his van and wanted to be on his bike.

We all left and went to the next bar and Irish took off. Convinced he wasn't going to come back, we sat around out front of the second bar telling The Outsiders what had transpired, but Irish pulled up on his bike. He looked like he was expecting to get his ass beat because he had layers and layers of clothes on. He looked like the marshmallow man. Members from all three clubs took Irish for a little walk down the road and let him know how we felt about him meddling in club business and starting rumors. It was a hard learned lesson, but he was able to ride home, and shortly after he left, the police showed up. No one was arrested and everyone went home that night. The next day, I contacted Quicky John and let him know we all felt Irish was an informant, and he denied even knowing him or asking us to contact him. And I thought that was the last we would see of Irish.

But I was wrong. After I'd established the Mongols in Oregon, he attempted to come back around. He started back with the same drama and what this club was saying about that club, stuff he had done before. Although Coconut Dan, for reasons only apparent now, was trying to get us to let Irish join, we never did. He eventually moved back to the Bay Area and didn't have much luck there. Due to still having Mongols tattoos, he was stabbed by a group of Hells Angels leaving a concert in San Francisco. He survived that long, but he was stabbed again by another Bay Area club a few months later. He ended up dying alone in a dark parking lot.

Coconut Dan was the first Mongol I had ever met. He lived in Carson City, Nevada near my cousin, and I would see him around town pretty often. Dan was pretty well-known in the area. He couldn't read or write, but he was tough as nails. He owned a tree trimming business, but his main passion was doing strength and martial arts exhibitions to promote Christianity for at-risk youth. He got his name because he would crush a coconut with his bare hands. He would also punch through bricks of ice and large cinder blocks. People were scared of Coconut Dan, and after being a Mongol for a few years out of Reno chapter, it didn't take long before he joined the World chapter as the Sergeant at Arms. He was the guy World chapter would bring to meetings with other clubs as a sort of enforcer. What none of us knew at the time was that Coconut Dan was a paid confidential informant for the ATF.

As a young man, Dan had wanted to be a police officer, but he had a hard time graduating from high school, and before long, he was charged with distributing cocaine. This killed his chance at joining law enforcement so he ended up working as a paid informant, first for the DEA and later for the ATF. Dan was an informant when he prospected for the Hells Angels in northern California before moving to Nevada and joining the Mongols. It was rumored that the Angels had tried to tell the Mongols Dan was an informant, but communication between those two clubs has never been that good, and who knows if they even wanted us to know. We weren't exactly friends. Dan spent years committing crimes and telling on those who did them with him. In fact, he was one of the main instigators of Operation Black Rain, the largest undercover investigation into motorcycle clubs in federal history. Dan was there in Florida when I flew out to meet Lars and the rest of World chapter. He was with us in Eugene when we rode around town during the Free Souls Anniversary party. In fact, Dan was scared to death that night and tried to order us to stay at the hotel. A few months after I had joined the club, there started to be issues with Lars, the president of World chapter. Dan was pushing hard to get Lars thrown out of the club, and we went to California to speak with the Mother chapter about it. I think Dan expected to replace Lars as leader of World chapter.

Another time, a close friend of mine invited us to come to LA. She was filming an episode of *Monster Garage* and they were debuting a new super-slow-motion camera that shot at such a fast rate you could see a bullet fragment on impact. They wanted to film Dan smashing coconuts. Our trip was cut short because Dan had gotten word that someone had shot up his house while we were in LA, and we drove through the night to get home so he could check on his house and girlfriend. We didn't know it at the time, but Dan had sent some local gang members to prison over a gun deal, and they had figured out he was a rat. After the Black Rain raids, the paperwork started coming out, and Dan was basking in the limelight like some sort of hero. He spent years assaulting people, instigating fights with other clubs, and convincing some of his closest friends to sell him firearms and thought that made him a sort of Donnie Brasco. Talk of him writing a book ignored the fact that he could neither read nor write, and it was also suggested he would be going on talk shows, but before he could take advantage of his fame, he died of a heart attack while up in a tree cutting limbs. I'm told his funeral was small. I don't think he was going to be missed.

The two Oregon informants were Lonnie and Odie. We had met Odie when we were still Vagos. He was a pretty active member of the Free Souls, and we would see him around at a lot of local events. What we didn't know was that he'd been arrested for stealing motorcycles, and, instead of doing his time, he chose to become a paid informant for the Eugene Police Department where he did his best to instigate crimes in return for a monthly paycheck. Odie used to tell us he got a military disability payment of $4000 per month and, looking back, it seems likely that was actually from the Eugene PD. Because he did this as a source of income, you can only imagine the crimes he tried to get others to commit or even make up in order to justify his income. Odie was trying to join the Vagos after leaving the Free Souls and, because we liked the guy, we ended up bringing him into the Eugene chapter of the Mongols not long after we started. Odie was proud to be a Mongol and went out right after joining and got the Mongol's 1 percenter diamond tattooed on the side of his neck. He talked about how proud he was to finally be a 1 percenter. He damn near slept in his patch. Looking back there were a lot of red flags. Things I should have recognized if I hadn't been naïve about informants. Because Odie was using meth and committing crimes, I knew there was no way he could be an undercover law enforcement officer. In fact, as a leader I had banned the Oregon members from using meth, and on two occasions, we took Odie to rehab to help get him clean and get his life on track. It pains me now to realize that all the while he was trying to build cases against all of us.

Odie was big into stealing motorcycles and often suggested we do it as a chapter. Every time he brought it up, I would shut it down. There isn't a lot of money in stolen bikes, and as a new club in the region, I knew it would just be an invitation for us all to get arrested. One of the worst aspects of remembering that time is what it tells me about just how corrupt some of our law enforcement officers can be. Odie was so determined to push through his plan to steal motorcycles that he drove to my place to talk about it. He was really pushing the idea of doing it as a chapter and putting the profits into the chapter treasury. I told him no, and never to bring it up again; we weren't going to do it. Several months later, when I was on probation and non-association from a kidnapping case I'll get to in the next chapter, an ex-member sent me some discovery paperwork from Operation Black Rain. It was a statement from Eugene Police Detective David Burroughs, the officer who was the alleged victim of my crime. The document made clear that he was Odie's handler. According to his statement, Odie had called me from the detective's office on speakerphone and asked me about stealing bikes and putting the money in the chapter treasury and that he had witnessed the phone call and that I had agreed to Odie's idea. There never had been a phone call; the meeting he was talking about had been face-to-face, and I had said no and not yes.

This would not be the first time Det. Burroughs lied to try and me put in prison. I guess someone had to justify the money they were paying Odie while he was the only one committing crimes. The weekend Odie received his full patch, we were in Carson City for a big party. A documentary called "Masters of Mayhem about Billy Queens" an undercover investigation into the Mongols in the '90s had just aired on National Geographic, and one of the old-timers who was with us made some sort of comment about what would happen if a member was found to be a snitch. Odie turned green and went outside. I went out to check on him and he was breathing heavy and all sweaty. He said he was really questioning if he wanted to join something that was so serious. Another time we were in Redding, backing up the chapter there. We decided to spend the night, and when we decided who would sleep where, Odie drew the short straw and went by himself with a Redding member who lived way out in the country. Next day the Redding member told me that Odie had acted really strangely, repeatedly asking where they were and where they were going and being really fidgety. Looking back on it now, I can see he'd probably convinced himself he was figured out and was being driven out to the woods for the last time.

In the end, Odie was kicked out of the club because of his drug use and run-ins with the law over stalking his ex. We hadn't seen the paperwork on him yet, we had no idea he was an informant, but he was no longer a good fit for the club so we kicked him out. About a year later, I ended up back in Lane County Jail for a probation violation. This was shortly after Black Rain and I had returned home from San Diego after being on the run and turned myself in for a warrant for absconding. During my trial, and after violating probation, I was sent to Lane County Jail and held in a single cell for twenty-three hours per day. On this particular visit, Odie ended up being in the cell next to me. He was there for violating a restraining order against his ex. Because he was in the cell next to me, we would get our dayroom time together, and I would often walk with him and listen to him cry about his relationship and how he didn't deserve to be in jail and spent most of the time trying to calm him down and just be an ear for him. He was no longer in the club, but we had some shared experiences that I thought made us friends, and I was just trying to help him. He asked me about coming home and why I turned myself in and I said, "Well, I'm hoping the judge revokes my probation. Then I can do my time in here, and come off probation and not have to deal with non-association anymore." When I was called in to see the judge for my probation violation hearing, Detective Burrough took the stand and reported that he had a confidential informant "in California" that reported that "Mooch said he was hoping to get violated and do his time in jail instead of probation so he can get out of probation and non-association." I may not be the smartest man, but I can remember what I said to who, and when I got back from court, Odie was long gone. It wasn't long after that that I ended up looking at that discovery listing Odie as Confidential Informant (CI) #2. Odie later ended up in prison due to continuing to commit crimes and eventually covered up his Mongols tattoo. During his time as an informant, I was the only Oregon member arrested for a crime. Odie was arrested more than anyone he ever informed on.

The second Oregon informant was Lonnie. Lonnie, too, we met when we were Vagos. He was the bouncer at a local night club we frequented and some of our friends worked. He was a big guy, covered in tattoos, and looked like a professional fighter. He didn't talk much, but he looked the part and had asked about riding with us and hanging around more. He ended up joining the Eugene chapter of the Mongols. Like Odie, he had a drug addiction and was often in trouble with the chapter for using. Lonnie was an informant for the ATF. Before moving to Eugene, he was an informant against the Vagos in the Sacramento area and relocated for his safety. He wasn't a very active member of the Eugene Mongols chapter, but we later learned he would record our chapter meetings and let law enforcement know how many members we had, what we talked about in our meetings, and stuff like that. He tried to sell members steroids a few times and eventually started trying to buy guns. He was so pushy about it that it made the members uncomfortable, and he was eventually kicked out of the club. Immediately after the initial Operation Black Rain raids, there was a temporary injunction that made it illegal for any member of the Mongols to wear or possess anything that said Mongols or Mongols MC, or had the clubs logo on it. As the chapter sarge prior to getting kicked out, Lonnie was holding the chapter's patches when he reported he was raided, and the Feds took them all. During this time, since they were not allowed to wear patches, members would wear black shirts that said "MFFM" or "Black and White Nation." Counterfeiting a shirt is easier than counterfeiting an actual patch, and Lonnie was making MFFM shirts and giving them to local drug addicts and bums in the Eugene area. These guys would be arrested for some charge no Mongol would ever commit, and then it would be reported to the papers that a Mongol in Eugene had been arrested for armed robbery or possession of meth etc. During his short time in the Mongols, Lonnie and his, who was not a member, got several Mongols tattoos. At some point, Lonnie had asked a member, Billy, to lend him some money. Billy gave it to him, and Lonnie insisted Billy hold on to something of value of Lonnie's as collateral. Billy insisted it wasn't necessary, but Lonnie pushed the issue enough that Billy gave in. Both Lonnie and Billy were convicted felons and banned from owning firearms. Lonnie gave Billy a pistol for "collateral." Shortly after Operation Black Rain, Billy was arrested for "buying" a firearm and possession of a firearm and, due to his previous charges, was sentenced to fifteen years in federal prison. All because he thought he was lending money to a "brother" in need. The Feds ended up changing Lonnie's name and moving him to a new house for witness protection. While there, Lonnie's neighbor found out his wife was sleeping with Lonnie and ran Lonnie and his dog down with his pickup truck. The dog died and Lonnie was severally injured. Not long after that, Lonnie's son took his own life.

If you had told me criminals and drug addicts were paid thousands of dollars to fabricate crimes and tell on their friends, I probably wouldn't have believed you. But that was my naïveté–I only knew about actual undercover law enforcement officers and didn't know there were such things as informants. Because we were not a criminal organization and weren't selling drugs or making money illegally, I never thought we'd have to worry about undercovers. But I didn't know that there are people out there whose sole income is the business of being criminals while telling on those around them. Nor did I know that there were cops whose sole interest was in putting people away, whether they had committed offenses or not. I was brought up believing in the essential honesty and fairness of the American justice system. I lost that belief with a certain amount of sadness.

CHAPTER SEVEN

THE EASY RIDERS BIKE Show is a regular event that travels around the country. The time I'm talking about, it was in Portland. The Gypsy Jokers, the Free Souls, and the Outsiders were there, and so were Hells Angels from Washington.– They still had their agreement that Hells Angels couldn't be in Oregon, but their relationship with the Gypsy Jokers was now pretty good, given their warlike history, and they got along together well in Washington. The ex-Mongol, Irish, was also there, and I had my say about him, but at this time, we hadn't yet found out that he was a paid informant.

We'd been given plenty of warnings, and not just by the FBI, that the other clubs were not going to allow the Mongols into Oregon. Well, we were going to be in Oregon whether they wanted us or not, and we figured the Easy Riders Bike Show was a good opportunity to make that clear. We'd present ourselves in front of all those other clubs. It would be a clear statement of intent.

Before that, though, we'd show them a different kind of lesson. At the bike show and every other big event, they'd be there in huge numbers, but that wasn't how they lived the rest of their lives. What we decided to do was to show them that, if they wanted to have beefs with us, they were going to have them as part of their daily lives. So, for example, we found out that a couple of Gypsy Jokers used to go to the same bar pretty well every night. Okay. So I'd start showing up there with four or five guys. Another guy rode his motorcycle to work the same route every day. I started following him. We went to an MMA fight and there were five Jokers there; we spread ourselves out around the place so that we looked like a lot and then, when they got on their bikes to go home, we followed every one of them. That made it look as though there were five carloads of Mongols following them. We weren't (necessarily) looking for a fight; we wanted to get across the message: You can live in peace with us, or you can live at war with us, but we are here and were not going away. Your choice. But make sure you understand that, if you want to have issues with us, it won't just be an occasional thing; it's going to change your whole lifestyle.

On one of our missions in Portland we got a call that a Gypsy Joker named Ryan was hanging out at a popular music venue in downtown Portland. We had two carloads of Mongols driving around, waiting for such an opportunity, so we went down there. When we arrived, he was standing outside, talking to the bouncers, and we watched from across the street while I tried to formulate a plan, but before I could, he got on his bike to leave. While it was warming up, I radioed the other car and told them we would follow him from a distance, see where he went, and call them if any opportunities presented themselves.

We followed him through town without him noticing. He was on a custom chopper, and I think he may not have had mirrors because he seemed oblivious to us. When he pulled into a gas station on a dark side street, this seemed like our best chance. We parked in the parking lot next to the gas station right above it and radioed the second car to come up behind the pumps but to stay out of range from the pump cameras. But we missed out again. As we pulled on our masks and exited our vehicles, I heard his bike fire up and rip out of the gas station. He hadn't been there to get gas; he'd just made a quick stop to talk to the pump attendant. Since we were already out of our vehicles, I approached the attendant and the others just followed my lead. I had a short talk with him, knowing he would likely call Ryan and let him know he was being followed and that two carloads of masked men just about got him. I figured this would prove my point, but we got back in our cars and ended up catching up to him just as he was pulling into the Jokers' clubhouse.

I parked a block away with a clear view of the building while the other car roamed the perimeter, checking for cops or other club members. Then we came up with an idea that, looking back, I'm glad we didn't follow through with. I say we came up with it because something strange goes on with twins—we can find we remember the same event from a totally different perspective; I think Jeremy suggested it and he thinks I did. Whichever of us it was, if we'd gone through with it. I don't think our relationship with the Jokers would be what it is today. Not to mention both Lonnie and Odie were in the second car, so we'd have been ratted out from the outset. I could tell Odie was getting nervous that we were about to do something so he got on the radio and said there were several cop cars in the area. We decided to leave. I'm not going into details about what the idea was, but in hindsight, I'm glad Odie made that call. A lot of things would be different today had he not.

Over the years, our relationship with the Jokers got better. We didn't really go to the same bars as them, we never took any of their ex-members, or hang arounds as members, and we generally stayed out of their way. I'm not going to imply they do any sort of illegal business, but we weren't doing any, so we also were not taking money out of anyone's pockets. These were points I often brought up when sitting down with bigger clubs as I started Mongols chapters in new areas over the years. As time went by, we were invited to some of the Jokers' runs that were open to the public. We even went to a funeral for Joker Jason inside the Salem Jokers' clubhouse. In 2016, the Mongols Salem and Keizer chapters built a new clubhouse in Keizer, and on a winter night almost nine years to the day after the Mongols first appearance in Oregon, the national president of the Gypsy Jokers and the national president of the Free Souls both sat down with a select group of Mongols to break bread in the new clubhouse. It marked the first time a Joker or Free Soul had ever stepped foot in a Mongol clubhouse. As I mentioned before, the Jokers are a very formidable foe, but I was much happier having them as friends. To this day, they remain a very serious and well-respected 1 percenter club.

We also decided to show ourselves to the Free Souls. I rounded up all the members in Oregon as well as some from Nevada. Unfortunately as it turned out, that included Coconut Dan, Odie, Irish, and Lonnie which, though I couldn't know it at the time, meant that the law enforcement agencies were receiving a running account of what we were doing. We went to a hotel near the Free Souls clubhouse, and then to a strip club that was even nearer. We didn't ride to the clubhouse; we were just making an appearance. We rode around making sure they knew we were there. Then we stopped at the hotel and had some lunch and that was the first time I was approached by people from the ATF. Looking back, it's obvious now that they were there to protect Coconut Dan. A black Ford Explorer turned up. This same black Ford Explorer had shown up to the scene at the second bar after Irish was beaten up a year or so earlier. The cops said it was a witness and kept going back and forth, talking to the Explorer's occupants. Call me naïve, but it took me a while to put this together, probably because I didn't (yet) understand the extent to which the law enforcement agencies were prepared to massage the evidence to match what they wanted. The fact was, the ATF had been present after Irish was assaulted, and they were here now. In any case, a guy got out of the Explorer wearing a jacket with the ATF logo. Walking toward me, he wasn't at all the military type I would have expected; this guy was out of shape and looked a bit like a dad. In a southern accent he said, "Well, well, well . . . What's going on here, guys?"

We don't really talk to law enforcement, largely because we've found you can't believe a word they say, but I heard him out. He said other gangs were out "Mongol hunting" and they'd just pulled some over and found firearms and ammunition in their trunk. "We know they are there, we know they are looking for you guys, so we strongly suggest that you stay at the hotel tonight." I went back in and talked to the guys, and the only ones who were really scared were Coconut Dan and Odie. Dan made a really big deal about not leaving the hotel. We already had plans to go out and hit some of the bars that the Free Souls would be in, and we didn't feel like giving that up because some ATF guy we didn't trust told us we should. We took a group vote and decided we were doing it. We called the Redding chapter and asked for backup as they were the nearest chapter, although they were still about five hours away. They asked whether there was a big police presence, and when we said there was, they declined to get involved. That was disappointing after the many number of times we had come to their aid, both as Vagos and Mongols, but what is, is. We got on our bikes and rode to every Free Souls bar in town. All we did was walk into a bar, make sure we were seen, have a couple drinks, and then leave and go to the next one. Coconut Dan seemed terrified all the way through, but nothing happened.

That was a way of telling the other clubs that we weren't scared, even when we knew they were looking for us, and it went together with all the other things we were doing to let their members know we weren't looking for trouble, but if it came to it, we knew where they lived, we knew where they worked, we knew what their favorite bars were, and if we had to, we'd upset every aspect of their lives.

Then I took a group of guys to a swap meet in Portland. We drove up in cars so they wouldn't see us coming, but we all wore club T-shirts. We put support shirts on some of our friends from the skinhead scene so that we looked like we had more members than we really did. We walked in and came face-to-face with Gypsy Jokers. Mark, who is now in prison for murder, met us at the door. We had a bit of a conversation and, essentially, I told them the same thing I told the Free Souls: we were a different kind of club from them, and we attracted a different kind of people. We weren't in competition.

On the other hand, we also weren't going away. They could accept us in peace or they could try to prevent us getting established and it was entirely up to them. I think that resonated with Mark. It was tense for a while, but it worked out.

Then I flew to Denver for the biggest swap meet in the country. Every club in the country goes there. The Denver Mongols picked me up from the airport, and I stayed with one of their members (who later turned out to be an informant and was involved in the Black Rain operation). The moment we arrived at the swap meet, a sheriff served a restraining order on us, saying we weren't allowed to be within a given distance of a Hells Angel T-shirt booth. That kept us apart all weekend.

When I got home, I found that things were still tense with the Jokers. We were going to a bar not far from their clubhouse, and I'd posted security outside. I learned a lesson that day about not posting security on their own, because we left a prospect outside with a walkie-talkie in case anyone showed up, and another prospect on the other side, but they couldn't see each other. Someone walked up to the first prospect, punched him in the face, and said, "This is Gypsy Joker territory." He lost his walkie-talkie, he was waiting for help to turn up, but we didn't know anything was happening. I also posted a car near their clubhouse because I wanted to know if they left there and looked as though they were coming to us, but they'd noticed the car. In fact, they'd noticed that we'd been watching them for a few days. The result was that their national boss called me and said it was time we met. I told him what bar we were at (which, in fact, he already knew) and he came down on his own, which impressed me.

We talked for half an hour and he made it clear that he knew where my parents lived, but it wasn't a threat. What he wanted was an agreement that, if things didn't work out, we wouldn't go to each other's houses. We'd sort it out between ourselves, but we wouldn't involve anybody connected with us. We agreed that, and from then on, things were all right between us. I wouldn't say they were cool with us being there, but they'd accepted it. Nowadays, Mongols and Jokers in Oregon get along pretty well, and it all started when that Joker boss had the balls to come on his own into a bar occupied by a number of Mongols. I had never met him before then, but I was impressed after meeting him and, honestly, I liked the guy. I could see why he was a leader.

Next up in the 'peace or war' negotiations was Brother Speed. For anyone who doesn't know, Brother Speed is a motorcycle club that started in Boise Idaho in the 1960s and is now active in Oregon as well as Idaho. They had history with the Mongols because members of Brother Speed were there in Laughlin in 2002 when the Mongols and Hell Angels had their very public shoot-out. Although Brother Speed wasn't involved in that incident, it did cause a conversation between the two clubs and where they stood with each other. Brother Speed has a long history of being friends with the Hells Angels, and most Mongols would interpret that as meaning they weren't friends of ours.

I couldn't see things that way. When I joined the Mongols, I knew what I was signing up for and what beefs I was inheriting, but I've never assumed friends or other clubs needed to pick sides simply because I decided to. It never made sense to me to hate on a club for who they were friends with. As long as they kept their peace with us and showed respect when we were around, who cares? Plus, no one likes a bully. I look at it like this. Had the Mongols told Brother Speed to pick a side, that would have given us one more enemy. But if we let them do their own thing and stayed out of it, they might not become an ally, but at least we could coexist and be cordial.

Things weren't cordial with Brother Speed when we first opened in Oregon. Like the Outsiders and Gypsy Jokers, Brother Speed didn't have any chapters in Eugene so they were less concerned about us being there, but they were concerned about us opening in Portland. And we weren't going to forget that the car that was pulled over when out "Mongol huntin" contained presidents of the Jokers, the Outsiders, and Brother Speed. So we had some clues about how they felt about us being there.

So, when not long after that night in Eugene for the Free Soul anniversary, the national president of Brother Speed requested a sit-down, I accepted but planned for what could be a hostile meeting. They picked a small strip club in Portland right next to the Ross Island Bridge. It was tucked away on a dark side street with only one entrance into the parking lot. We got there early, in cars so no one would see us coming. I had a scout watching their Portland clubhouse to let me know when they left and how many people they had. In the meantime, I parked two cars near the exit to block them in if needed, and two cars in the back corners of the parking lot with the trunks popped and a man behind each car, if things got out of hand. Three of us sat at one table and the other three at a nearby table.

Brother Speed showed up on bikes, and there was only three of them. When they walked in, the atmosphere in the small bar drastically changed. You could tell the patrons were scared. We ended up having a good talk, much like the ones I had with the Free Souls and Jokers, I let them know we wouldn't be taking any of their ex-members and wouldn't be frequenting their bars; they requested, after our presence in Eugene, that we would not attend their events uninvited. We shook hands and they left.

We had a tense moment with them one time after that, at another strip club. We bumped into each other while we were leaving, and they were arriving, but things ended peacefully and we continue to coexist cordially in the same state. They even have a few longtime members that I have stayed in touch with over the years and consider my friends. I first met one of them when I was prospecting for the Outsiders. He saw me standing guard outside and came up and said, "Didn't want to give the winged skull a chance, huh?" In effect, he was asking why I didn't chose his club, but I always remembered him from that moment, and we have stayed in touch to this day.

That left one more club to sit down with: The Portland Outsiders. By now I am sure the clubs had been talking about how we had been conducting these sit-downs. I wasn't going to do anything any different with the Outsiders as the method had worked well so far. We were prepared for this one to be a little less cordial since there was a shared history, and I imagined some of the beefs with them were likely personal since I left their club and then came back and started a new club in their backyard. I didn't do it to be disrespectful, but I could understand why some of them may have taken it as disrespect. Either way, I was anticipating some hostility.

As usual, we got there just over an hour early. This particular bar was pretty close to their clubhouse and a regular spot for them. As we got there, I recognized one of their older members in plainclothes; I assumed he was scouting the place. We do the same thing, but I found it odd they chose to use someone I knew and would recognize. As soon as we walked in and spaced ourselves around the bar and exits, he got on his phone. The spotter I had watching their clubhouse notified me they were heading our way, and there were a lot of them. When they funneled into the bar, 'a lot' turned out to be more than a dozen. Their Portland president was hard to communicate with that day as he was visibly upset, but thankfully their Tacoma president was a voice of reason, and we were able to have a respectful conversation.

The Outsiders have been in Portland longer than any of the other Portland area clubs, and they fought a lot in those early years to call Portland theirs. Where most of the other clubs wore a bottom rocker that read "Oregon" theirs read "Portland," and they were not happy about us wearing a Portland side rocker, so I made a concession, and ended up making the same agreement as I had with Brother Speed. In order to coexist and respect both clubs history in the area, we would change the name of our Portland chapter to "Rose City." Not only was it Portland's nickname, but it paid homage to my roots in the Rose City Bovver Boys. I gave them my word, shook hands, and then we left. I called the Mongols Mother chapter secretary and promptly ordered new side rockers that said Rose City to honor our agreement.

Later, after a leadership change, the club's new international president, Lil Dave, didn't like how the name Rose City sounded and suggested we change it, but I am a man of my word and fought to keep it. Unfortunately, after I moved to California, Junior, an old time member now in charge of overseeing Oregon for Mother chapter, decided he didn't care about any agreements I had made and allowed the Portland chapter to switch back to their Portland side rockers. Time had gone by, and fortunately the change didn't cause much trouble with the Portland clubs we had made the agreement with, but it saddened me as it made it look like I had gone back on my word. I'll have more to say later on the terrible leader Junior turned out to be.

The Mongols still are, but definitely were then, a very California-centric club. Most of their concern has always been California politics and relationships with California clubs. When the members heard of the issues we were having in Oregon, they'd say things like, "They can't stop us, we are Mongols," or "Don't they know who they are fucking with?" And while the Mongols were a larger club nationally than the existing Oregon clubs, we were greatly outnumbered in Oregon. Not only that, but these clubs were not some Ma and Pop groups. The Outsiders and Jokers fought a very bloody war with each other in the 1960s and had a violent history with many other clubs. They deserved to be treated with respect and taken seriously. I was happy that we were able to sit down with them and come to some agreements. Although we didn't become friends right away, we did all learn to coexist.

CHAPTER EIGHT

IN APRIL OF THAT year (2008), I was arrested. I'd already had some experience of how far the law enforcement agencies were prepared to go to fit people up and get convictions for offenses that had never been committed, but even so this one took my breath away. Of course, fifteen years later, we have all had a close-up view of just how willing the American press is to present distorted and untruthful stories to back up their particular view of how the world ought to be, even though it isn't, but it still seemed fairly new in 2008. Now that we have a legal scene in which the Speaker of the House of Representatives can say that the purpose of a trial is to give the accused a chance to prove his innocence rather than to give the accusers a chance to prove his guilt as we were taught from childhood, I think we all know we're not in Kansas anymore.

At the time, I was prepared to accept that I'd been the victim of an unfortunate series of events. I realize now that the whole thing was, from start to finish, a deliberate program of entrapment by law enforcement officers without an honest bone in their bodies.

My parents' house was very much off the beaten track and set in 150 acres. In the same 150 acres was a little house where Jeremy and I would stay. I was driving a pickup truck away from there one day when I saw, coming toward me on my parents' driveway, a black Ford Explorer. I knew we had an arrangement with the Jokers that, if things broke down between us, our houses and the houses of people close to us would be left alone, but you can never be sure. Even when the IRA and the Police Service of Northern Ireland agreed to cease hostilities on the signing of the Good Friday Agreement, there was still an offshoot of the IRA that kept up the bombing, the knee-capping, and the killing. How did I know that there wasn't a small part of the Jokers unwilling to accept the deal I had made with their leader? I didn't, not for certain. So who was this driving toward me on a private driveway in the back of beyond with tinted windows so I couldn't get a clear view of who was inside? I could see the outline of two people, but I couldn't see who they were.

When they saw me coming, they stopped. I stopped. I was watching them closely, wondering who they were, what they wanted, and what was going to happen next. But then they started to back up, they turned round, and they drove away.

If I had simply let them go and gone on my own way, what happened next would not have happened, though now that I know who was involved, I strongly suspect they'd have done something else to get what they wanted. In any case, I still needed to know who they were. I was driving away, leaving my parents' house unprotected. How did I know they wouldn't turn round and go back there when they knew I was out of the way? So I decided to follow them.

When we reached the end of the driveway, I had intended to turn left and go north. I would wish many times that I had done so, but when they turned right and headed south, I did the same. I still couldn't see who they were, but I did know that they kept looking back toward me so they knew I was there, and I did know that they were doing a lot of talking to each other. I followed them for about ten miles until we reached the interstate. They got onto the interstate and turned north, and that was very strange, because if they had intended to go north, they would have turned left when they left my parents' driveway and not right. Now my suspicions were really aroused. What were they doing? Were they trying to circle around and go back to my parents' property now that they knew I wasn't there? I realize now that I was being led by the nose by two men whose sole objective was to get me into jail whether I had done anything wrong or not. I wish I'd realized it then, but at that time, I still had some faith in the American justice system. I didn't yet understand that their aim was not to arrest the guilty, but simply to arrest.

I tried to get alongside them to see who they were, but they prevented it. They raced, they switched lanes, they did everything they could to keep me at a distance. And then they took an exit which, as it happens, was the exit for the Gypsy Jokers' clubhouse. When they did that, they achieved what they wanted to achieve; they convinced me that they were Gypsy Jokers and not the cops they really were.

To get to that clubhouse meant driving down a series of little cul-de-sacs and side streets and I wasn't going to do that on my own, so I parked at the gas station from which I could see the clubhouse. Sure enough, they parked in the clubhouse driveway. Now I was certain: the men who had visited my parents' house were either Gypsy Jokers or they were Hells Angels or members of some other affiliated group. What other explanation could there possibly be? The guy in the passenger seat cracked his window open just enough to get his hand out and point his fingers at me shaped like a gun, so that removed any doubt; they knew I was following them. I needed backup. So I got on the phone. I called Jeremy, I called Little Zac, I called some other people for support.

While I was doing that, the black Ford got back on the road, and this time it headed south on the interstate. Why? Were they heading back to my parents' house, knowing I wasn't there? I already knew they weren't going to let me get alongside them if they realized I was following, but what about Jeremy? If he pulled alongside them in a vehicle they didn't know, it would simply look like someone overtaking them, and he would have a chance to see who they were. So that's what we did, arranging it all on the phone.

I followed them for about sixty miles, during which they were dodging in and out of traffic, speeding up, slowing down, pulling all kinds of stunts. I was convinced they were members of another motorcycle club, and they saw us as enemies. As we got closer to Eugene, which is where our chapter was, I called ahead and got two other guys to meet us on the interstate in cars and not on bikes. Unfortunately, as it turned out, one of the guys I called was Lonnie who was, of course, an informant–so now, though I couldn't know it, the ATF and the cops knew everything we were doing and were able to trap us even more thoroughly. And what they also knew for certain, because Lonnie was able to tell them, was that the only reason I was following them was because I thought they were renegade bikers who wished me or my family harm. They could have stopped this at any time. They could have rolled down a window and said, "Hey, Mooch, we are the Feds. We are not enemies. We were checking you out. Go about your business and don't be so suspicious." In fact, it was brought up in my trial that Agent Packard had my cell phone number and could have called me at any time. But that would not have gotten them the prize they wanted, which was bodies in jail. When you run paid informants, you have to show that you are getting something for your money. Removing the concerns of a citizen who isn't actually doing anything wrong doesn't cut it. You need arrests, and above all, you need convictions. Never mind that the guy didn't do anything–get him sentenced. And make sure you have a tame reporter on board to tell the public your side of the story and suppress the other guy's.

We agreed on the phone to try to get a car in front of them and a car behind them and then to put another car alongside them so that we could actually see who was driving and who was the passenger. Of course, we didn't know that Lonnie would be able to tell them what we were doing, and so it was a bit of a surprise when they suddenly shot from the slow lane to the fast lane, and when they did that, they turned on the siren. Then they turned on their lights. When they did that, everyone took off except me. Just before turning on the lights, they had jammed their way over to an exit, and I had gone with them. At the first opportunity, I turned on my turn signal and drove into a shopping center parking lot. I wasn't concerned; I hadn't done anything wrong. I came to a halt in the parking lot, and so did they, facing me. They didn't get out of their car, and so I didn't either. We sat there staring at each other. Then I looked in the mirror and saw about two dozen cops surrounding my car, guns drawn. I kept my hands up so they could see I wasn't a threat. The cops opened my door, dragged me out, and handcuffed me.

Then out of the black Ford Explorer that had started all this came the same ATF agent who had approached us during our visit to Free Souls territory. He said, "Well, well, well." Then—and I only know what was said from the trial transcripts I saw later—the cops walked up to Packard and let him know their dash recorders were on. Then they turned up their radios so the recorders couldn't hear what was being said. Packard said to me, "Well, that was quite the game of cat and mouse. What were you doing?"

I said, "What were YOU doing?"

"Oh, I don't know, I was just seeing how long you would follow me for." He was smiling and joking around. He said, "I can't imagine you guys broke any laws, but the cops are going to want to take a look at you so just hang tight and they'll cut you loose."

The cops hadn't even known that Jeremy and Little Zac were there, but they had followed us around and were watching from another parking lot. My aunt had come down and was getting everything on a camcorder. The cops put me in the back of a police car, and I felt like the president of the United States with police motorcycles providing an escort in front and behind and running every light on the way to the jail. When we got there, I was in a single holding cell while they rounded up some of our other guys, but they refused to talk without an attorney. I, on the other hand, wasn't by any means sure that the ATF guy had been truthful in the parking lot, and I knew that, if I was interrogated, the interrogation would be recorded, and I wanted that recording to happen.

I let them see I was going to talk to them openly, but I concentrated on asking what they had been doing. I said, "Why were you guys trespassing on my property?" I used that word 'trespassing' a few times because I knew they wouldn't want it heard in court.

He said, "Oh, we were doing an investigation and we wanted to verify where you lived."

"So why didn't you identify yourselves?"

"Oh, we didn't feel we were in any danger. We just wanted to see how long you would follow us. We were going to drive on until we ran out of gas." All of this still with the laughing and joking attitude, like nothing was serious. But what I really wanted was for them to admit what they were doing, and I did well enough at that that they kept the recording of this interrogation out of my trial. My attorney wasn't allowed to bring it up, and it wasn't played, which is pretty strange behavior for law enforcement officers because the whole point of an interrogation is so that the court can hear exactly what was said.

They said they were going to charge me, Nathan Cassidy (a Mongols prospect), and Matt Weiss (a friend from Unity Skinheads) with attempted assault. Who we'd attempted to assault, they didn't say, but in any case, I thought with a charge like that we'd be out in the morning, and if it even came to trial, any decent attorney would be able to get it thrown out. So we were held in jail overnight and taken into court in the morning. They dealt with us separately, and when I saw Nathan and Matt come out of court, they looked like they'd seen a ghost. They were white. They slid the paperwork under my door. Charge One was conspiracy to commit kidnapping. Charge two was attempted kidnapping. They hit me with a litany of insane charges. My bail was initially set at $14 million and reduced to $1.4 million at a bail reduction hearing. Obviously, the result was that I stayed in jail the entire time I fought this.

My family helped me get a really good attorney. I was in jail for sixty-three days, the trial was just over a week long, and the ATF agent who had been so friendly and joking sang a different tune in court. Describing his conversation with me after the cops told him their radios were on and then turned them up so they couldn't hear or record what we were saying, he said, "I was in fear for my life. I thought these guys were going to run us off the road. We were so concerned, we even had our guns unsnapped. I was so angry after we got into the parking lot, I still got to Mooch and said, 'What the hell were you doing? You tried to run us off the road. You had us in fear for our lives.'"

This was a turning point for me. Of course, ever since I'd seen the charges I'd known they were trumped up, but I had no idea just how far they would go. These were law officers and to realize that American law officers were prepared to lie on that scale shocked me. We are taught things in school from our earliest days about what America stands for and what makes it the greatest country to live in. It's still the greatest country to live in, but so much of what we have believed is simple fantasy.

State law says, if I make you go in a direction you don't want to go in, I'm kidnapping you. In fact, I hadn't made them change from one thing to another, but they said I had, and they said that amounted to kidnapping.

We were all offered plea bargains. Nathan and Matt took theirs, but I already had a felony recorded against me, which would put me a lot higher than them on the sentencing guidelines, so I refused. Matt pleaded guilty to coercion and got thirty days in jail; Nathan pleaded guilty to reckless driving and unlawful use of a weapon (his car) for which he got ninety days. The plea bargain they offered me was for two years in state prison.

When it came to trial, I was so glad I had such a good attorney. I don't want to think about what happens to people accused of things they haven't done who either can't afford good representation themselves or don't have a family able and willing to pay for it. My brother testified for me, and the police claimed that he was lying because they hadn't known he was there. We pulled my phone records and his phone records and we were able to show that he had not only been there, but he and I had been in contact the whole time. Then my mom testified. The prosecution was doing this big number about how the Mongols were criminals of the worst kind–to listen to them, you'd have thought you had to be subhuman to get into the Mongols. So my mom stood there in the witness box, an Italian-American mother and a highly regarded schoolteacher, and gave the court a different idea about these people who were being maligned. "These people have been to my house. I've heard all the things people say about them, and they just aren't like that. Of course I wasn't happy at first, I'm a parent; I don't want my child breaking the law or doing things that are dangerous, but now I've met these people. I know them. They are my son's friends and they're just like any son's friends. To me, now they are like family."

Then Detective Burroughs and Agent Packard testified. Packard was the agent who had handled Coconut Dan and Lonnie, while Detective Burroughs was a local policeman, but he was also the head of the Outlaw Motorcycle Gang Investigation Unit, a national organization, and he was Odie's handler.

I was found guilty of reckless driving and menacing, and not guilty of all the important charges like conspiracy and attempted kidnapping. Those are misdemeanors and not felonies. You only had to look at the judge to see her fury that my attorney had shown law enforcement officers to not be credible, and she wasn't able to hit me with a really big prison sentence. What she gave me was a year in jail followed by five years of probation during which I would not be allowed to associate with any member of the motorcycle club. We tried to fight that, particularly given that my twin brother was a member, but the judge wouldn't listen–the only time I would be allowed to associate even with Jeremy would be if we were spending time together during Christmas or Thanksgiving. Otherwise, we'd need the approval in advance of my probation officer.

As it turned out, I was violated four times for hanging out with Mongols. Looking back, of course, it's clear; they knew the hangouts had taken place because they had informants in the club. Every time I was with a club member, at a bar, say, or having a meal somewhere, or just shooting the shit, Detective Burroughs and/or Agent Packard would get a call saying, "Mooch is here," and I'd find them sitting outside in a car. I'd wonder, *how the hell do these guys always know I'm here*, though now I don't wonder anymore because I know.

Burroughs and Packard were nothing if not vindictive. I suppose you can see their point; they had to justify the cost of paid informants, they'd been sure they could hit me with a big felony, and all they'd gotten for their trouble was a couple of minor misdemeanors. One time, we'd taken our girls out for a Valentine's dinner, no one was wearing club stuff, it was nothing to do with the Mongols, but next day Burroughs and Packard went into the restaurant and asked for all the receipts in an attempt to show that I'd been there with someone I shouldn't have been there with. When Operation Black Rain went down, my mother's house was the only one that had all the doors smashed in and who should be raiding it? Detective Burroughs and Agent Packard. Later, after I graduated, I moved out to Illinois. You might imagine that the cops would be pleased that someone they'd been hunting all that time had decided to turn his life around by getting an education and a job. You'd be wrong. Detective Burroughs did everything he could to get me fired from my job and kicked out of school. At one point after all of this, Jeremy and Megan separated for a short time, and she moved back to stay with her parents in Carson City. Agent Packard and Detective Burroughs went to visit her at her parent's house and tried to tell her Jeremy didn't care about her or his family and that he was talking to other girls. They tried to convince her to testify against him. She declined, but it shows how far these two continued to go.

CHAPTER NINE

FOR SIXTY-THREE DAYS, I had been held in a single cell for twenty-three and a half hours each day. My meals were served in the cell and I didn't get any recreation time at all. I was allowed out by myself to make a phone call or take a shower and then escorted back. I had been offered a plea bargain of two years in prison, and I was looking at a lot more than two years if I was found guilty. I was so tired of being in county jail in these circumstances that I even considered the plea bargain, but I knew the charges against me were bogus, and I was determined to fight them. And in the end, I was glad I did that. The judge was obviously as keen to get me a heavy sentence as Detective Burroughs and Agent Packard were, but when the evidence was put before the jury, they understood what had really been going on. I imagine for some of them it must have been a shock to realize how unscrupulous–in fact, how completely dishonest–some people in the American justice system can be. And I don't kid myself; if my family hadn't been both ready and able to pay for a really good attorney, I'd have gone down. That's what happens to a hell of a lot of people in America who don't have the money to defend themselves. They end up serving long prison sentences for crimes they didn't commit. In some cases, crimes that no one committed. We need much greater awareness of that in this country.

I was in the news a lot, and I know that because they would bring me out of my cell and let me watch myself on the news. I was found guilty only on the misdemeanor charge. The jury reached that verdict on a Friday, and I was told I'd be brought back into court on the Monday for sentencing. I thought by now I knew just how devious and dishonest the people I was dealing with could be. I was wrong. The normal practice would have been to take me straight back to jail. That's what had always happened. Not this time. They put the cuffs on me, and then with a guard in front of me and a guard behind me, they took me down some stairs and through a tunnel I hadn't even known existed. When we came up again, we were in a parking structure. They put me in a police car and then they put a second police car in front of me and a third behind me. And that's how we went back to jail. I said to the guard with me, "You do know I was not guilty?"

"Yeah," he said. "But we were afraid your guys were going to try to bust you out."

Of course, that was a lie. They knew no one was going to try to bust me out for a misdemeanor, heck, we wouldn't have tried that even if I was looking at twenty years in prison. And they knew it. But it was just part of their endless campaign to pull the wool over Joe Public's eyes. At one point in the trial, they'd had twenty uniformed cops in the courtroom when I was brought in. What do you suppose the jury thinks when it sees that the accused needs to be surrounded by that many armed police? And when my attorney objected, the judge said they'd received information "from a credible source" that the Mongols were going to try to break me out. Suggesting that a judge lied could get me into serious trouble, even now, so I prefer to stick with the idea that it was the police who had lied; they had told the judge this rubbish and the judge had believed them. The "credible source" was Detective Burroughs and Agent Packard, and they have as much credibility as an ice cream cone in a nuclear explosion.

Of course, it's all about appearances. They had it in for me because I belonged to a motorcycle club and the police didn't like motorcycle clubs. Note this: the chapter I belonged to had committed no offenses. We just liked being a motorcycle club. But for the cops, we had to be presented to the public as public enemy number one. They didn't miss a trick. One day when I was in jail, the jail went into lockdown and another prisoner told me, "They're going to blame this on you." I just laughed, but sure as shit, they let it be known that a Mongol had ridden round the jailhouse, and they'd had to call the bomb squad when a suspicious box was left outside. Not a word of this was true. And then on Monday, I was taken back to court to be sentenced.

Usually, given the overcrowding in American jails, the sentence for my kind of misdemeanor was a slap on the wrist. Probation. I confidently expected when I went into court that morning that I'd be going home. Instead, the judge gave me the maximum sentence she could. One year in county jail.

By this time, I was starting to wish I'd taken the two years in prison instead, because (and I know how ridiculous this sounds), there's a lot more freedom in prison than there is in jail. I was filling out forms, hoping to qualify as a trustee, which would get some time off my sentence when a guard came in to see me. He asked what I was doing, I told him, and he said, "Oh, forget about that. The jail is overcrowded. Just hang tight and we'll cut you loose."

What went on now was just an extension of the justice system's foolishness up to this point. County jails have a matrix that grades offenses by seriousness, and depending on where your offense sits in that matrix, says how much of your sentence you actually do. My offense was reckless driving, so how many months out of my twelve did anyone think I was going to do? A normal person sentenced to a year for reckless driving would have been out in twenty-four hours, but they used me as a political example. The jails were overcrowded. They needed bigger jails, more jails, and more guards. And look, the problem was so bad, they were going to have to let someone as dangerous as me back on the street! Detective Matt Herbert was quoted in the *Oregonian* as saying, "It's a sad commentary on the sad state of the criminal justice system in Lane County right now." It certainly was, though not in the way Detective Herbert meant. If it hadn't been me, I'd have laughed. I did see the funny side, but laughing was beyond me at that point.

I had to sign an affidavit that I was going to do a couple of months of road crew in lieu of my remaining jail time. As soon as I got out, I'd have to turn up Monday to Friday, sign in, and spend the day out on the road, picking up trash and doing all the other stuff American citizens have become used to seeing to keep the road network from collapsing. This was part of my one-year sentence, but I was able to go home every night, sleep in my own bed, eat my own food, and it was way better than spending a year in county jail.

The morning I was about to be released from jail, there was a big buzz from a number of cells with guys saying, "Look out your window, man. There's something big going on." When I did look out, I saw the place was swarming with cops. And with photographers. The front of the building was surrounded. Now, I may have an ego, but I never for a moment imagined that that was for me–I'm just not that important. But it was. It was all part of the campaign to tell the public that the jails were so underfunded they had to let a vicious criminal like me go free. So when I got downstairs, I said to the deputy, "Look, man, I've been in jail for sixty days. I don't want to go out of here and be on the news. So let me leave by the back door, okay?"

They did that, but I didn't have access to a phone to call for a ride, so I just ran. I ended up in downtown Eugene, and of course, I have a problem because I'm on probation and I'm not allowed into bars, but bars are where the public phones are, and I desperately needed to make a phone call. At that time, they were still selling physical newspapers on the street, and I could see a newspaper with my photograph on the front cover saying I was being released. So people knew who I was, or if they didn't know who I was, they knew what I looked like. I thought, *My probation could be over before it even starts if someone sees me walk into a bar and calls it in.* But I took the chance, my aunt came down and picked me up, and it worked out fine in the end.

In fact, I ended up doing my year because it was a condition of my probation that I couldn't associate with anyone from a motorcycle club, and I was violated four times for doing exactly that. Of course, what I hadn't known was the extent to which we had been infiltrated by paid informants. And they snitched on me. For example, the Eugene chapter put together a barbecue for me, and they did it at the place of a member who lived way out of town. We thought, *No one is going to find us out here. And what will we be doing wrong? Nothing. Eating steaks and drinking beer. All-American pursuits since forever.*

Each time I was sent back to jail, I was there for one or two months. And I was young, and I hadn't been a Mongol for long, and I didn't want to stop being a Mongol. And I thought, *Hey, I'm on misdemeanor probation.* It's not like I was a lifer out on license where they watch you like a hawk. If I left the state, no one was going to send a posse to bring me back. I wasn't that important. And the cost in relation to an offense of reckless driving would have made it ridiculous.

A guy, Big Mike, who'd been in World chapter and then been in Oregon with me for a while, had moved down to San Diego and he'd offered me a room to rent if I needed it. He was opening up a tattoo shop down there with another Mongol and they'd offered me a job. It was actually Big Mike who'd tattooed Mongol on the back of my head. He was a tattoo artist and his original plan had been to open a tattoo shop in Oregon. He'd invited Jeremy and me to join him as business partners, and we thought that was a good idea because it was a way to be fulltime Mongols and still have a job that brought earned income. The only problem was we didn't have any money, so my aunt lent us $5000, which we gave to Big Mike, who promptly took off for San Diego. Obviously that could have caused trouble, but he said if I was there with him, he would give me money each month to send back to my aunt until the $5000 was paid off.

Before I went, I had a going away party. Lonnie was there. It was the first time I'd ever seen him with a camera, and he was taking all sorts of photographs, not just of me but every member. Later, of course, when we knew he was a paid informant, we realized that he hadn't been taking those photos for his own personal book of memories; they were for the cops who paid him.

Then my mom drove me to the airport and as I was going through the metal detector, I saw this guy who looked like something out of a movie. He was looking straight at me and talking into a walkie-talkie, and I thought, *Surely to God, this can't be happening.* Everywhere I went in the airport, this guy was behind me. I got to my gate, I sat there, he walked away, and I looked over and saw another guy with a newspaper up to his nose, ear piece in, and he was watching me. I thought, *They're not gonna let me get on the airplane.* But they did. I can see now that they just wanted to know I was gone, but at the time I had to change flights in San Jose, and I was thinking they were going to arrest me for violating parole by leaving the state and I would do my time in San Jose, which would be far worse than in Oregon because in Oregon I had family.

None of that happened. I got to San Diego, I didn't see any cops looking at me there, Big Mike picked me up and took me back to the house, and I ended up living in San Diego for a while. I worked in the shop doing cleanup, learning how to be a piercer, and at the same time, I was learning how to be a Mongol. San Diego was a dangerous place to be a Mongol–the first two Mongols to be murdered by Hells Angels died there, and the relationship was still bad. It wasn't much better than a war zone. If Mongols wanted to go to a bar, they needed to go mob-handed, they shouldn't stay too long, and we had a group of nonmembers we called The Wrecking Crew who were in charge of our security and driving the chase vehicles when we went out. So I learned a lot about security, basic procedures, and protocol.

I also got to know LA pretty well; that's where our Mother chapter was and we spent a lot of time there. There was a place in LA called The House Lounge that was owned by a Mongol and was big enough to get all the California Mongols in it.

It was at a party there that I was approached by Hollywood. He'd been a hang around at the Denver swap meet and now he was a member. He told me he was gonna be in Oregon soon, so I said, "Cool, man, what do you need? You want to hang out with the guys? Where are you going to be?"

"Either Eugene or Portland."

The first red flag about that was that Eugene and Portland are about one hundred miles apart. He said he was going to be up there for work, so I said, "Well, I assume you know where you're working." But, what the hell, I said, "Well, if you need anything while you're there, let me know and I'll put you in touch with someone who can help."

He said, "No, man, I need some armed guards for a transaction that is going down."

If not knowing where he was going had been a red flag, this was a much bigger one. He said he would pay the guys; he needed four men and he'd pay them $2000 each. He said, "I'll just give you the $8000 now and you can make the arrangements."

Now, I know I may have been naïve in letting guys who were paid informants pull the wool over my eyes, but I wasn't in any doubt about this one. I mean, I didn't know this guy from Adam and he walks up and starts proposing illegal shit to me? If he wasn't a cop working undercover, he was certainly working for one. I said, "No, man, I'm not interested. We are not into stuff like that."

I walked away from him and told the guy running the chapter, "That guy, Hollywood. He's a cop." And I called Jeremy and I said, "If this guy calls you, don't even talk to him."

It turned out Hollywood's real name was John Carr and he was an ATF agent. But before we found that out, there was an incident at a funeral for a Mongol who had been shot; the first Mongol to have been killed in quite some time. Jeremy was there, and Hollywood approached him. He made the same pitch as he'd made to me and got the same response, and then he asked Jeremy whether the Oregon members carried. Now, there's no open carry in Oregon, and no one with a felony charge against him (like me) will ever get a license, but if you don't have that charge against you, pretty well anyone can get a license to carry. That meant that pretty well all the Oregon Mongols legally carried firearms, and Jeremy told him that.

When Jeremy told me that Hollywood had brought up the money again, I told the people who needed to know and, this time, they decided that his membership needed to be brought to an end. This took place at the funeral home, after which we were going to the cemetery, and at the cemetery, we would pull his patch and send him down the road, making it clear we wanted nothing more to do with him. But he must have realized that his time was up because he didn't turn up at the cemetery, and in fact, we never saw him again. Then, two days later, Operation Black Rain concluded and eighty-eight Mongols were arrested across six states. The paperwork later stated that Operation Black Rain had had to conclude early because "Mooch from the Mongols had identified John Carr as an undercover agent and Carr had to be pulled out for his own protection."

The charges were based on racketeering and said that we were using the patch for personal gain or for criminal enterprise. The result was an injunction preventing us from wearing the patch and, in fact, it was illegal even to possess one. In California, if members had "Mongol" on their motorcycles, the Feds took the bikes. They took their vests, they took all their personal property.

All the legal stuff going down was what enabled us to find out that there were four undercover agents embedded with us and too many paid informants to count. The result was that no one talked to anyone else because no one knew who they could trust. My chapter was gone, everyone I worked with in the tattoo shop was gone, my roommates were gone, I had nowhere to stay, and no way to earn any money.

I ended up staying with my aunt in Yucca Valley, a desert town out past Palm Springs and a bit of a hillbilly place if I'm being honest. (Sorry, Yucca Valley residents). A Mongol called Gaucho would pick me up at weekends and bring me to his house in Riverside. I spent a lot of time with him and his family and got to know them really well. But I had to accept that life couldn't go on like this so, right after Christmas, my mom and dad picked me up and drove me back to Oregon, and I turned myself in. Gaucho was having a birthday party, there were all these serious gangsters around the place, and the announcement went out over the prospects' radios, "Mooch's mom is here to pick him up." That caused some raised eyebrows and got a good laugh.

I was back in jail and hoping just to get violated. What I wanted was to do my time so I wouldn't have to do five years' probation afterwards. But the judge was onto that, so she worked off one count at a time.

Anyways, I did my time, and when at last I was out of jail, I stayed with my mom, and–inevitably–I started thinking about what I was going to do with my life. It took a while, but eventually I would have a goal, something I wanted to achieve. All I had to do then was to invest nearly a decade of my life in turning the idea into reality.

CHAPTER TEN

AFTER ABOUT THIRTY DAYS, I was back home in Oregon. The day I was released, I called my Aunt Joan for a ride. She told me that Jeremy and Megan's first child, Olivia, had been born that morning, and we went up to meet her and the family.

A lot had changed in the club during that first year. Doc, who was international president at the time I joined, had written a book, gone on *Gangland* and some other TV series, and decided to step down as president. He had suggested at a president's meeting that he hand pick his own chapter that essentially wasn't going to answer to the new IP and kind of do what they wanted as well as oversee Mother chapter. The club's members didn't agree with Doc's idea and he retired. It didn't take long to find out that Doc had been stealing hundreds of thousands of dollars from the club and his status was changed to out bad. When Doc stepped out, Mother chapter's Sergeant at Arms had stepped in as acting president until elections, but Black Rain hit shortly after that, and he and a lot of members of Mother chapter were arrested. With everyone else arrested, the Mother chapter's secretary/treasurer stepped up to fill the international president position until elections.

This was a tough time to be in leadership. A lot of the main guys in the club had been arrested, the club wasn't allowed to wear their patches, and no one trusted anyone else. Not the best time to take the reins. At the next election, Lil Dave was elected as the club's next international president and he built the new cabinet of

officers within Mother chapter. Doc was the main defendant on the
RICO indictment against the club, and it didn't take long before
he agreed to work with the government and turn rat against his
former club. Before leaving the club, Doc had taken the club's federal
trademark and changed the registration to his name so, on paper,
he owned the rights to the Mongols MC images and logos. Part of
his plea agreement was that he forfeit this trademark to the federal
government, which he did. That whole case, the forfeiture of the
Mongols patch, has resulted in a legal battle that is still going on to
this day.

Back in Oregon, Jeremy, Lil Zac, and I kicked off the Salem
chapter, the Mongols' third Oregon chapter. Not long after that, we
started the first Washington chapter in Vancouver, Washington. We
put a lot of focus into growth during this time, and once we had
our patches back, things expanded pretty quickly around the state.
Jeremy and I wanted to start a support club to help guys who didn't
have club experience or wanted to be in a club but weren't ready to
take the big step into a major 1 percenter club. I spoke with Lil Dave
about the idea, and he told me about a support club that already
existed in Oklahoma called The Raiders. Dave said he would prefer
that I get with Oklahoma Jeff, who was in charge of the Raider
program out in Oklahoma, and figure out a way to make it something
we could grow around the country. That way, we would only have to
manage one official support club instead of a lot of different ones.
So I started speaking to Jeff, and together we developed the Raider
program. Jeff was an old-school and well-respected member of the
Mongols. He had been shot and paralyzed as a prospect in the '70s
and had gone on to be a very important Mongol in that region and
nationally. We got really close working together, and later, when I
was looking at colleges to transfer my associates degree to, I strongly
considered Tulsa just to be closer to Jeff. Due to the club politics of
Oregon, and thinking ahead to states that had Gypsy Jokers and
Outlaws, I suggested we change the Raiders' patch colors from black

and white to gray and black. Jeff absolutely didn't want to do this and was pretty upset when we rolled out the first Oregon set, and they were gray. But things were going a lot better with the Jokers, and I didn't want to reignite any potential issues, so at the time I thought this was the best play. Jeff and I took old, original, Mongols bylaws and updated them to fit with the Raider program and then we began to roll it out.

At the time, there was one Raider in the entire country, and he was in Oklahoma. We started first in Oregon and Ventura, California. To have a Raider chapter in your state, an existing Mongol chapter had to sponsor and oversee them, so it was very similar to the Mongols in the way of structure, security, etc. Lil Dave put me in charge of helping Mongol's chapters around the world start their own Raider's chapters. Eventually the Raiders had chapters all over the US, Australia, Thailand, and even Russia. As the Raiders expanded, we eventually changed their colors back to black and white. A few years after getting the program started, Oilpan, a member from Spokane, even updated and redesigned their center patch to the patch that is worn today.

What really ended up working out well was that a lot of guys who joined the Raiders, after some time, realized what they were doing in the Raiders wasn't much different than the Mongols, and over the years, a lot of Raiders stepped up and joined the Mongols. In Oregon, Jeremy and I started chapters in Keizer, Linn Co., Mid Valley, and Millerburg with Raiders who wanted to step up.

I was continuing to spend time with the club and staying active during this time and found myself back in jail often for violating the terms of my probation. My fourth time in Lane County Jail, the sheriff's officer told me he had lost a bet. He hadn't thought I would be coming back. I spent most of that last stretch, just under two months, considering where I was in my life and what changes needed to be made so that I would stop this revolving door. I was going in and out of jail every few months and that was no way to live.

Here I was, twenty-eight years old, with no real marketable skills. Leader of a motorcycle club wasn't really meant to go on a resume.

During my school days, I was really into photography and music. When the other kids in high school were deciding their careers and their future, all I could think about was moving to Portland and playing music. During high school, I got a job at a photography shop called The Shutterbug. I would package and ship orders and make sure each store in the state had inventory on the floor. But one day, the police came in with a warrant for my arrest for an assault, and The Shutterbug didn't want me back after that. Once I moved to Portland, I started working at The Hot Topic, which was fun but hardly a career. I ended up quitting that job to focus more on the band. I worked at another retail store for a bit, then pumped gas, worked at a grocery store warehouse for a very short time, and then started work at the porn store.

I started out as graveyard shift security. Places like these get robbed often, and it was my job to deter robbers and stop people stealing from the sales floor. I worked my way up to manager and the day shift. I worked there for close to five years before moving to Nevada. In Nevada, I started as an electrician's apprentice but moved to the gas company once they were hiring. I spent a season installing electronic read transmitters on gas meters around town. It was a good gig but temporary. Then I went to work at the local Harley dealership selling motorcycles, but that job relied on weekend sales, and I was often taking weekends off to ride with the Vagos so it didn't last too long. I switched to a metric bike shop and worked in the parts department, selling parts for dirt bikes and ATVs, until I moved back to Oregon. In Oregon, I went to work for a Vago named Slider, who taught me how to lay tile, and I ended up working with a team on a big job building Sacred Heart Hospital in Eugene. Magpie, who was also a Vago at the time, worked with me. When the job grew, we both became in charge of making sure all of the tile teams had the materials they needed and spent most of the time driving back and forth between the hospital and the warehouse.

We spent a lot of time together, but when I left the Vagos and things got a little hostile with them, I decided it probably wasn't the best place for me to work. That's when I put all of my time and effort into growing the Mongols and being the best Mongol I could be. And where did that get me? Sitting in jail. I had worked at some tattoo shops over the years. I worked for Sacred Art Tattoo with my skinhead friend, Joey, who got me into riding Harleys. And when I absconded from probation and moved to San Diego, I worked at a tattoo shop that Mongol Mac and Big Mike owned. But Mac and Mike were arrested in Black Rain, and things weren't going good at the shop. Mac was arrested first and, while he was locked up, Big Mike, the same guy who took money from my family and never paid it back, opened up credit cards in Mac's name. Things were going downhill fast. Big Mike and I were not getting along. I had started looking into his story and found that pretty much everything he had told us and the club about himself and his past was a blatant lie. I had to recognize that I wasn't going to get back the money he owed my family and I cut my losses and left the shop.

So here I was in jail, going over my job history and realizing I was close to thirty and had no marketable skills. No career aspirations. But I did know one thing: I did not want to stay on the path I was on. I wanted to prove that deputy right; I wasn't ever going to come back here again.

A Mongol out of Hollywood chapter went by the name Richie Rich. Richie was covered in tattoos, a big, bearded, muscular man who looked as though he'd just walked off the prison yard. His tattoos went up his neck and down his hands, and each finger had a big ring on it. He was an intimidating looking character, but once you talked to him, you realized he was a kind and genuine man, as long as you didn't cross him. Richie was also a doctor, with a PhD in Clinical Psychology, working in drug and alcohol counseling. One of the things he did was to go into prisons and work with the inmates. After speaking with him, I decided this was a career I would like to check out.

Finding a career when you're heavily tattooed and have a felony criminal record can be challenging, especially when you've been all over the news, but this seemed like a field where my history might actually benefit me. I looked into it and saw I was going to have to go back to school. I had tried college in my early twenties, but with no direction, no motivation, and no goals. I went for one day, hated it, and said I would never go back. But this time was different. This time I had focus. I knew what I wanted to do and what I had to do to get there. So I went back to school.

I started with the goal of getting my two-year degree in addiction studies and then working toward becoming a certified drug and alcohol counselor but, as I progressed with school, I fell in love with psychology, continued for my bachelor's degree in social and behavioral studies, and eventually got my master's degree in social work. In the end, it took me eight years, but I kept my promise to myself and never went back to jail again.

I started at Chemeketa Community College in Salem. In California, I'd met a girl on social media named Shawnta. She lived in Portland and had recently gone through a breakup and we spent a lot of time talking on MySpace. I had moved to California without a motorcycle. While I was there, a brother from Old South Bay chapter, Simo, who had several, would let me ride one of his to club events and on rides etc. Shawnta had told me she had a Softail Heritage she had financed for her boyfriend at the time. It had been sitting in her garage since they broke up, and she was looking for someone to give her rides on it. Seemed like a great deal. Who wouldn't want to spend time riding motorcycles with a pretty girl, right? I moved home, and though she didn't really have the motorcycle, we began dating and ended up getting a little apartment together within walking distance of the community college. I was getting financial aid and student loans so I wasn't working. I was going to school fulltime and it was my full focus. I was getting a 4.0 each semester, was on the president's and dean's lists, and was accepted into some honor societies. I figured a felon with tattoos all over his body needed as many positive things on his resume as he could get.

Because I was doing so well in school, my probation officer didn't hassle me much. All of the informants were now gone, and when I associated with the club, I kept it pretty low key, but I was still active. After two years at the community college, about three years into my probation, I went to court to try and get my probation terminated early as it was keeping me from some of the internships opportunities I had in school. My probation officer was in support as I am sure by now I was pretty low on his priority list, but the judge denied our request.

I had saved some money and was looking for a cheap motorcycle I could rebuild. I found a wrecked Buell 1125R on Craigslist. It was salvaged and the seller wasn't asking too much; in fact, he was willing to sell it to me for half the price he was asking with the promise I would pay the other half in a few months. We wrote a quick sales slip and the promissory note, shook hands, and I was back on a bike after almost two years. I had no way to get it, but brother Rambler offered to take me to pick it up. I had first met Rambler in San Diego when he came into the tattoo shop looking for Mac. He explained he was a South Bay hang around and was about to fill out his prospecting application with Mac. At the time, Dago had more of the younger members and, apart from Mac, South Bay was mainly older guys, so I couldn't understand why a young dude like Rambler would want to be in Old South Bay and not Dago. In fact, that is probably why I even remembered him.

Shortly after that, the raids hit and I didn't see Rambler for some time. One day out of the blue, he hit me up. He was a full patched member now and he had accepted a job in Portland for a while, helping a landlord fix up older houses and sell them. He would live in the houses as they were being fixed and then move on to the next as they sold. With his outgoing personality and quick smile, it didn't take long for him to be a popular guy both within the Oregon Mongols and at the local bars and strip clubs. Rambler was really enjoying Oregon. Coming from San Diego where you always had to have security and be on point, Rambler often said that Oregon was like Disneyland. We had smoothed over relationships with the local clubs by then, and he could freely wear his patch wherever he went. Rambler was buying an old pickup truck from another member and offered to take me to go get my new bike.

We spent the day together and talked of all the things we were going to do with this bike and how we were going to fix it up. We planned to work on it together when Rambler got back from San Diego. He was going to drive back down there, pack up the rest of his stuff, and make his move to Oregon a fulltime one. I wish I had known that the day we spent driving around, talking about motorcycles and the future, was going to be the last day I ever saw him. When Rambler was back in San Diego to pack up and move to Oregon, he was confronted by two Hells Angels at a bar. Rambler was out with his girlfriend having dinner and left the bar to go somewhere else, but the Hells Angels followed. He was stabbed and killed in the parking lot of a taco shop in front of his girlfriend. He was one day away from being out of San Diego for good, but he didn't make it. The Oregon Mongols continue to do a memorial run in his honor called The Rambler Run in March of every year.

CHAPTER ELEVEN

So THERE I WAS, in community college, living with Shawnta, and just starting on a two-year degree in drug and alcohol counseling, which was the whole of my objective at that time. But during the course, I began to fall in love with psychology. I graduated the two-year course with a 3.9 GPA, and I'd begun to accept that I needed the strongest educational outturn I could get to offset the things stacked up against me. Shawnta had got pretty heavily into alcohol, and neither alcohol nor drugs has never been a big thing with me so that relationship had come to an end. It makes me smile now, but one day when she was at work, I had my mom come and pick me up. Twenty-eight years old, a convicted and time-served felon as well as a Mongols chapter president, but when I needed help, my mom was who I turned to.

My probation officer needed to know where I was because he did quite regular home visits to check that I was observing the nine o'clock home curfew that was part of my probation, so I told him I'd moved into my parents' basement. I knew I didn't want that as a long-term goal, and most of what I was doing at the time was working out where I wanted to go to school, so it needed to be somewhere else. I started applying for different schools around the country.

At the same time, I had just started a Spokane chapter of the Mongols. FSU were a group from the punk rock hardcore scene. FSU originally stood for Fuck Shit Up, but as they grew and became better known, they changed it to Friends Stand United. The guys who had started that gang in Boston, as they aged, and mostly joined the Outlaws in Boston, but there was also an FSU group in Virginia Beach that I had come to know quite well. One of them was Gabe, who used to hang out with us in the Rose City days. When I was in the Mongols San Diego chapter, they had been starting a Virginia Beach chapter. They didn't have many members; in fact, they'd started out with two; one had been a Navy Seal who was found out during Black Rain and thrown out of the military, and the other was busted when he sold a gun he's brought back from Afghanistan to an undercover agent. So I linked the Virginia Beach FSU with the Virginia Beach Mongols and they all ended up joining. That was the beginning of a link between the younger generation of FSU and the Mongols.

There was still a group of FSU in Spokane and I became really tight with them, especially with Weedy, Oilpan, and Eddie, an MMA fighter. They wanted to be Mongols so I talked to Lil Dave. At that time, Junior was overseeing Washington and Oregon for the Mongols so I had to clear it with him. Junior at that time was pushing hard for a truce with the Hells Angels. He'd spent some time in prison with a high-ranking Hells Angel, they'd become friends, and a truce was something he really wanted. So the Mongols' Mother chapter was doing a lot of sit-downs with the Hells Angels and what we were trying to get was a sort of cordial ceasefire. The Hells Angels were well established in Spokane; they'd been there since the eighties and it was a historical place for them. It's very close to the Canadian border and the Hells Angels are strong in Canada. I'm not going to imply that anything illegal was going on, but if they needed to cross the border in either direction in a hurry, they wanted to be able to do it.

Well, we ended up getting approval to start a Spokane chapter, but it wasn't long before things kicked off with the Hells Angels. They had a confrontation downtown, and Junior put out a message to every Mongol in the Northwest: "We have to get up to Spokane right away to support the members there."

I was on non-association, not allowed to leave the state and not allowed to associate with Mongols, but you don't ignore a call like that from the leadership, so I snuck out of my parents' house late at night and a bunch of us drove up there. When we got to Oilpan's house, we were regrouping, trying to figure out what was going on, and I kept saying, "We have to wait till Junior gets here. He's in charge, he'll figure out a plan." But Junior didn't arrive, so I called him, and he said, "Oh, I'm not coming; there'll be too many cops." I couldn't believe it. I had all those reasons not to go, but he had called, and I had ignored them. I was missing school and risking being returned to jail, to do what Junior asked me to do, but Junior wasn't prepared to do it himself.

Oilpan had a tattoo shop, so while we waited for other people to arrive, we went to the shop so I could get a tattoo. There were cops everywhere. The place was crawling with them. They clearly knew what was going on. So I'm in the basement, Oilpan is preparing a drawing to tattoo my neck, and the Raider who had driven me to Spokane came running down the stairs. "Feds! Feds! The Feds are everywhere!" The FBI had come into the tattoo shop, trying to prevent the gang war they had been told was about to break out, and here I was, on non-association and not allowed to leave Oregon, and I'm down in the basement with no way out.

The ATF agent asked for Oilpan, so Oilpan went up there, and the agent said, "We know you have Jeremy from Oregon up here so we are keeping an eye on you guys." I breathed a sigh of relief at that; they thought I was Jeremy. I called Jeremy. "Apparently, you're in Spokane. Don't leave your house, don't go anywhere, don't be seen, don't let them know it's me." And soon after they left, I got in the car and went home. That night, a bunch of Mongols went to a bar, a bunch of Hells Angels went to another bar across the street, and every cop in Spokane stood in the middle of the street to make sure nothing happened between them.

One of the things this did was to show Lil Dave how serious the Hells Angels were about us being in Spokane. David got mad at Junior for green lighting a Mongol chapter in a town that was solidly Hells Angels and, because Junior is the guy he is, he had said he knew nothing about it. "It was Mooch, acting on his own. Mooch never told me there were Hells Angels there; he said it would be easy." Much against my wishes, Lil Dave closed down the Spokane chapter; the only time in all my experience as a Mongol that we closed a chapter because of the presence of another club. The members had to relocate–Oilpan moved to Phoenix, Weedy moved to LA, and Eddie moved to Utah.

And then I reconnected with Amber, a girl I'd known in high school. When I was a junior, Amber had been a freshman. She and I had not gotten along in high school. I'd dated her best friend, Christal. As I've already said, I wasn't popular with everyone in high school. The skinhead look may be in now as a fashion statement, but it was seen very differently back then. And tattoos, which I started getting when I was sixteen, also made me something of an outcast. So I was the bad kid and Christal's dad was a retired cop and she went to Bible study after school each day. Her parents would drop her at Bible study each day, I'd pick her up, we'd hang out, and then I'd drop her back there. Amber saw me as a bad influence and didn't care much for me.

Then, years later, while I was getting ready to go back to school, we started talking on social media. MySpace? Facebook? I can't remember. Amber had an identical twin, and I am an identical twin, we both went to the same high school, and as we started talking, things worked out the way they so often do. She would come over and stay with me and I would go over and stay with her and we fell pretty heavy. We started dating and I told her I was applying to different colleges.

Amber was at Western Oregon University, studying to be a special education teacher, and close to finishing. I'd already been accepted by Willamette University Law School in Oregon, but I checked out schools in California–Cal State, UC Irvine, others. I was still thinking about going to Tulsa to hang out with Oklahoma Jeff, and I also thought about Old Dominion University in Virginia to be with the Virginia Beach guys. In the end, I went to Whittier College in California. They had an amazing psychology program and small classes, and Whittier was near LA in the heart of Mongol country.

Amber still had one semester to go at Western. We got an apartment in Los Angeles and moved all our stuff in, but then we were apart for six months. When she graduated, she moved in with me.

I'd had to go to court to get permission to move out of state, and at the same time, the judge had dropped the supervision order so I was still on probation, but no longer supervised. I was still not supposed to associate with Mongols, but now no one was checking. As long as I didn't get arrested for anything, the fact that I was on probation would never come up.

I had been trying to figure out what chapter I wanted to join when I moved to California. Richie Rich was in Hollywood chapter and, because he was my mentor when it came to school stuff, I thought about joining him there. I told Dave that, and he said that, after Black Rain, it wasn't what it had been. I'd met guys at the Heights chapter and hit it off with them, but when I told Dave that, he said, "Why don't you join Mother chapter?"

I saw that as a huge honor. I'd only been a Mongol for four years, and being invited to join Mother chapter wouldn't normally happen that quick. I probably didn't pay enough attention to what I was actually being offered. In fact, I was probably naïve. Mother chapter was the international leadership chapter and I assumed that joining it meant that I'd be back to being in charge of Oregon and wouldn't have to listen to Junior any more. Dave soon put me right, explaining that I was just a soldier in Mother chapter, I did not hold any office, and was not overseeing Oregon. That would come later.

CHAPTER TWELVE

THE FIRST SIX MONTHS in California without Amber were tough. I was thirty years old, going to a small liberal arts college with kids fresh out of high school. My family and most of my closest friends were in Oregon, and I was living in an apartment by myself. We talked every day and she would visit when she could. We got an airline credit card and tried to fly back and forth when we could. We were bummed I was going to have to spend Thanksgiving alone, and we hadn't seen each other in over a month, but a member of the Mongols Vancouver chapter, who was a pilot for Alaska Airlines, got me a standby flight during Thanksgiving. When I showed up to Amber's work the day before Thanksgiving, she was so happy, and so were my mom and family. By the end of the year, Amber had finished school and was finally all moved in with me in Los Angeles.

When I first met Needles, he was a member of El Monte chapter, but by the time I had moved to LA, he was with The Heights. Needles was an incredible tattoo artist. He owned a small tattoo shop right down the road from Whittier College called Self Made Tattoo, in Santa Fe Springs. Before Amber moved down, I spent most of my nights after school at Self Made. There were always other Mongols stopping by and hanging out, and this is where I really got to know and build great relationships with brothers like Big Balls, Chacho, Cholo, and Rabbit. Rabbit was a Mongol from The Heights chapter and became one of my closest friends while I lived in LA. If I wasn't at Self Made, I was often riding around bars in Fullerton and Brea with Rabbit. I have fond memories of my times at Self Made and the relationships I built there. About a year later, Needles was killed in a motorcycle accident, and the shop closed down. Those of us who spent time there all got the Self Made Tattoo logo in memory of Needles and those times. When a Mongol dies, he is transferred to what the Mongols call chapter thirteen. His name is read each week at every chapter's meeting as well as during roll call at all major events. It is a high honor in the Mongols to be remembered in chapter thirteen and only those in good standing are able to join. As time went on, Big Balls, Chacho, and Cholo all joined Needles and Rambler in chapter thirteen.

Weedy had moved to LA around the same time as I did, and we hung out a lot too. The more we hung out, the better I got to know Trinity, at that time his girlfriend and now his wife. I enjoyed hanging out with the two of them. Trinity ran an entertainment company, providing dancers for bachelor parties and other private events and needed a reliable driver. At the time, the only income I had was financial aid and a few hours a week entering data into a computer program for a research team at the college. Amber was working as a special education instructor at a school in Culver City and, with California's cost of living, things were tight, so I worked for Trinity on the weekends. I would pick the girls up, bring them to the party, meet the host, make sure he had paid the agency and we had all of his information, and then work as security during the party to make sure no one tried to touch the dancers or get out of hand. I would also help collect all the dancers' tips and carry the cash out of the party for them at the end of the night. It was a pretty chill job and I never really felt in any danger, although there was always an opportunity for problems to arise. Trinity's company was well managed, she vetted the clients before we went there, so not too many people would rob the entertainment when we had their full name and address, but when you are around a lot of cash and people have been partying, you never know. Being a felon, I never carried a gun, so I had to be extra cautious, but I believe the way I carried myself and the way I spoke to others often made everyone feel at ease. Thankfully, I never had any issues. I worked with Trinity until Amber and I moved back to Oregon. Without that job, I don't think we would have been able to afford to live in California. I heard later that the guy who took my position was shot and killed during a robbery, so it sounds like I left at the right time.

I don't, though, want to leave Whittier without saying some of the good things about it. Because there was a lot that was good–really, the only thing wrong with Whittier was that it was in such an expensive state. The college was active in promoting a community environment. They encouraged students to start clubs for whatever special interests the students might have. I was inducted into PsiChi, the national honor society for psychology, and I was elected vice president of the Whittier chapter. I also joined the Whittier psychology club.

If it hadn't been for my Mongols membership, I'd probably also have joined the Whittier motorcycle club. I was certainly invited. The only transportation I had in California was my motorcycle, and I rode it to school every day. One day I came out from class and was getting geared up to leave when I saw a note on my bike from campus security. I called the number on the note, and a security guard told me to stay where I was because he was on his way to talk with me. I had no idea what this might be about, but when he reached me, he started talking about motorcycles and asked how long I had been riding. I still wasn't sure where this was going until he said, "We are starting a Whittier College motorcycle club. We are going to meet up and plan rides and do local charity events. I was wondering if you would be interested."

Whatever I been expecting, it wasn't this. I thanked him, but said I was already in a club. He said, "Really? Who?" and when I said "The Mongols" his facial expression changed, he stepped back and apologized and he left. I wasn't asked to join any clubs after that, though I did join a photography club while I was there, and my research team presented a study we had worked on at the Whittier College Undergraduate Research Conference (WURC).

I really did enjoy my time at Whittier, and often regret that I didn't stay and finish my undergrad there, but Amber missed home, we were really struggling financially, and staying in California just wasn't in the cards. It's a great pity. I know I'm not the only person who has been priced out of Whittier and colleges like it, and I think everyone it's happened to regrets it.

In any case, I lived in LA for about a year. Apart from college, I was still a Mongol, and at the beginning, I was in Mother chapter, but I was regularly butting heads with Junior, and I didn't stay in Mother chapter for long. I got the feeling that Junior saw things as personal. He aligned himself with people who didn't get along with Jeremy, and there was a lot of pushback against Jeremy's leadership in Oregon. They wanted to undo the protocols we'd put in place over the years; one key issue was the deal I'd made with other clubs in Portland that we wouldn't wear a Portland side rocker. Junior decided to undo that, which didn't go down well with the other clubs.

The Vagos had told us southern Oregon was their area, and we couldn't have members there. Well, okay. But now the Vagos were telling Junior that they wanted to have a chapter up in our area, in the valley. My attitude to that was the same as Jeremy's; we'd agreed to stay out of their area and they must stay out of ours. For whatever reason, Junior didn't see it that way. We had told the Vagos they couldn't have the chapter they wanted, and Junior kept butting in and pushing hard for the Vagos to be allowed to have their chapter.

I think what it came down to with Junior was that he'd been in the club in the 1970s and he'd even been national president, but he was national president when the Mongols was a small California-based club with somewhere around thirty members. It was a very different club now. If you read his books, you get the impression Junior had left every time he got a new girlfriend, he left when he went to prison, but he'd come back, and it was important to him that people should be able to see that he had power. Being seen to have power was more important to Junior than having a motorcycle club that operated the way most of its members wanted it to operate. Am I saying he was something of an autocrat? Yes, I suppose I am. And an autocrat doesn't like being argued with. So it became something of a power struggle where the power was the thing that mattered. And to achieve that you need to do a lot of undermining.

Lefty and Junior had done prison time together, and it was through Junior that Lefty had joined the Mongols. Lefty and I had been pretty tight, but when rifts between Junior and me became clear, Lefty backed away from me. Between them, Lefty and Junior got Lil Dave to transfer me to Heights chapter as Sergeant at Arms after Rabbit, who had been Sarge, was away in Georgia for school.

Heights was the chapter I had wanted to transfer to in the first place, and even though Rabbit had gone, Needles were still there so for me it worked out pretty well.

One of our members was getting married in Reno. There was going to be a Street Vibrations event in Reno at the same time, a number of Oregon Mongols would be there, so I decided to ride up there on my own. Round about this time, I'd been talking a lot with a Vago called Jabbers who was thinking of joining the Mongols. Before I got to Reno, there was a whole bunch of Vagos there, including Jabbers, and they got into it in a big way with some Hells Angels. There was a shoot-out, a Hells Angel was killed, and Jabbers and some other Vagos were arrested. I got a message saying the Hells Angels were in Reno in numbers, they were pissed that one of them had been killed, and wearing my patch might not be the best idea. So I took it off. I was there to go to a wedding, not to get involved in trouble between two clubs who didn't get along with each other, and I was happy to be low key. There were a lot of Vagos when I reached Reno, and they weren't wearing patches either.

All the Mongols who were in town for the wedding were staying in the same hotel, which was owned by a Mongol. As I was pulling in, two Vagos were pulling out, and I noticed they were wearing patches. Then, as I got into the parking lot, I saw it was full of Vagos, all wearing patches, and they were cozying up to the Mongols. The plan was obvious; they were in a serious fight with the Hells Angels, they knew the Mongols were no friends of the Hells Angels, and so they wanted to be friends with us, at least for the moment. I got on the phone back to Lefty to make sure the Mongols weren't going to get involved with Vagos issues. As I stood there, the two Vagos I'd seen leave came back, this time with a car right beside them, and whoever was in the car shot them off their bikes right in front of us. Then they went on shooting; everyone else hit the deck, but I just stood there like an idiot. Three o'clock in the afternoon, broad daylight, and we'd just witnessed a shooting right in front of us.

The Vagos survived, but they had to go to hospital, and we Mongols had to mount up and ride to the wedding. I can tell you, it was pretty tense. Hells Angels were riding around town, looking for the people they had a beef with, and we were going to ride through town to a wedding. The wedding was in the backyard of a bar just off the interstate, so it felt like we were sitting ducks if the Hells Angels decided to have a go at us, but that didn't happen. The wedding went off well, there was a big party afterwards, but the surrealist atmosphere from when I stood, bemused, watching a shooting continued. One of the entertainers was a female fire dancer. Her boyfriend was there and decided to join in, and his whole head went up in flames. He was running around, trying to get someone to put the fire out, nobody seemed to know what to do, and I was thinking, *Hell, first I watch people getting shot and now I see a guy on fire; this is a hell of a visit.*

After the wedding, I rode back to California and Bang Bang, another Heights member, and I flew to Daytona for an East Coast run, the first time I'd been to Daytona since I met with the Mongols to discuss joining them. Our relationship with the Outlaws had improved a lot since those days, but now we were having issues with the Pagans, and Bang Bang and I had a few run-ins with them while we were there, nothing serious. When we got back to California, I sat down with Rabbit and talked about the possibility of setting up a new chapter for some of us younger guys, but it turned out he was already in talks about doing exactly that, and we did in fact start the new chapter, Fullerton. It turned out to be a hard riding chapter, but we started getting a lot of extra police attention because it was in a prosperous residential area. It didn't take the police long to find out that I was involved, and that I was on non-association. That was one problem; another was that it was summer vacation, our lease was coming up for renewal, and it was going up quite a lot.

I was still working for Trinity, but I needed to find another job as well just to make ends meet. Jamison, a buddy of mine from Oregon, came down to visit. We went to Disneyland and did all the California stuff, and whatever we did, Jamieson paid. He was making a lot of money. His father owned a catalytic converter company, and Jamison was one of the people he employed to go out and find converters. He gave me the pitch: If you want to come back, you could be doing this too.

Initially, the idea was to do it in California so Amber stayed while I went back to Oregon to get trained, but the California dream was coming to an end. Amber was homesick, California was becoming more expensive every week, and we decided to just move back home.

I had transferred into Whittier as a junior because I had those two years at community college, I had really good grades during the year I was there, and when I got back to Oregon, I started at Willamette University.

Willamette and Whittier were very similar schools. In theory. In practice, there was a huge difference. In Whittier, people had not made value judgments. As far as they were concerned, I was who I seemed to be – a hard-working honors student. That now came to an end. My second day at Willamette, I was at the bookstore, noting down prices of the books on my reading list, and a security guy took me to an office where I was treated like shit. I had no idea what was going on, and these guys were accusing me of stealing. I had no backpack with me, and I kept asking them, If I've stolen something, where have I put it? Eventually, they had to accept that I hadn't stolen anything and they let me go, but there was no apology. I talked to my school counselor about it, but I got nowhere. They'd looked at me, they'd seen the tattoos, they'd drawn their conclusions. It was a bad start. The classes were okay, but I didn't feel a connection with the material, the teaching staff, or the students the way I had at Whittier. I ended up transferring to George Fox University after only one semester, and that's where I was given a certificate of academic excellence, where I graduated, and also where I got my master's.

While I was at George Fox, I originally returned to Portland chapter of the Mongols to help them rebuild after most of the members who had followed Junior had quit. Then Jeremy and I formed a new Keizer chapter.

I carried on with the catalytic converter business for a while, and it was pretty good money, but I didn't really enjoy it. One aspect I really didn't like was buying used catalytic converters, often for a lot less than they were really worth. I know that's business; maybe I'm not made to be a businessman. I went back to selling motorcycles, and I went on doing that right through my time as an undergraduate and then in graduate school. The problem with that job when I'd first done it had been that most sales are at the weekend, and that interfered to an unacceptable level with my desire to be riding. Now, that wasn't such an issue. I was very heavily into school, we were doing a lot of local stuff and not going out of town very often, and I was no longer in that first stage of club life when I wanted to be in everything and go to everything and be the most active member I could be. I was focused on my relationship with Amber, I was focused on getting through school as successfully as possible, and the club was still important but no longer my first priority.

Amber and I were two months away from getting married. We had gotten engaged, we'd planned the wedding, we'd sent out invitations, but there was a difference between us that we were never going to be able to overcome. I didn't want children. (I still don't.) At first, neither did Amber, but that idea faltered. More and more, she wanted to be a mother. More and more, she raised the subject. More and more, it became clear that we were not going to be able to resolve this and, if we both wanted to be happy in the long run, we were going to have to get there separately.

I don't know whether I'd ever have had the courage to accept that it was over between us. Fortunately, Amber was brave enough for us both. I had gone to Thailand on Mongols business and when I landed, a text message was waiting for me telling me it was all over. When I got back home, Amber had left. We'd had the time in California, we'd had three full years in Oregon, we'd adopted an English bulldog, and started fostering for a local bulldog rescue, and now it was over.

I said good-bye to 2015 with mixed feelings. I had expected it to be the best year of my life. I would graduate with my bachelor's degree, I'd go to Thailand, and I'd get married. It didn't work out that way. I did go to Thailand and I did graduate, but the time I'd hoped for was still two years away.

CHAPTER THIRTEEN

Before I left California, the Mongols had thrown out their national secretary/treasurer and Lil Dave talked about me for the position, but Lefty was against the idea. He and I had always gotten along well, but I think he knew it would upset Junior.

When I got back to Oregon, I found the Mongols in a bad way and Junior was to blame. The essence of the Mongol way of life is brotherhood. Wherever you are and whatever chapter you belong to, every other Mongol is your brother. You go on other chapters' rides. You support them without question when they ask you. That was the model Jeremy and I had done our best to put in place. Chapters went to events together, met up and rode together, stayed together, and essentially acted like one big chapter. Junior had done his best to destroy that model. The way he had them going, each chapter was completely independent. Some became very inactive. Some didn't support other chapters' events. And some chapters wouldn't even hangout with other chapters. This was not the Mongol way and was not what these brothers were taught when they came in. Oregon Mongols had been well-known for how structured, tight, and active they were, but under Junior, this was all falling apart. Old-timers like Peck and Junior were visiting the state and taking advantage of the hospitality always given to visiting Mongols (free meals, free drinks, rides to and from, whatever you needed), but all the while, they were spreading negativity, politicking against Lil Dave, and setting chapter against chapter. The state was divided into those who supported Junior and those who supported Lil Dave. But it wasn't just supporting Lil Dave, it was supporting the traditions and values the state was founded on. Between Junior not showing up against the Angels in Spokane, the agreements he was making with the Vagos without the clubs' approval, and going back on our word about Portland rockers, I think most members were starting to see who he really was.

After I moved back to Oregon, Lil Dave brought me back into Mother chapter and this time it was to oversee the Northwest. Lil Dave, Jeremy, and I had spoken often about how having local chapters overseen by out of state members (Junior lived in Utah) didn't make a lot of sense. Unless the member went to Oregon often, he would only know what weas going on by what he was told. And often, these guys would find one kiss ass who would make them feel important and would listen to no one else. So, together, we developed a new structure called the Rep program. It first started as regional reps, where for example a longtime member in Oklahoma would be a rep for the Midwest, a longtime member out East would be the East Coast rep, and so on. As the club grew, it developed to the point where most states had their own rep. The idea behind the program was that the person best suited for membership would be one with years of experience in the club and also in the area. State reps would be responsible for enforcing the club's commandments and constitution, making sure all chapters were getting along and representing all Mongol standards, for resolving any instate disputes, and for relaying information to and from Mother chapter. Another thing we learned after the issue with Junior and the Vagos was that someone local is better suited for sitting down with local clubs as they have a better idea of local politics and the local landscape. Something that works between clubs in California may not work in Oregon or Oklahoma. Every state has different clubs, different politics, and different leadership. The rep program went really well, helping the club grow outside California while also helping it stay more structured. The Mongols saw a big change in support for out of state runs and events when a rep was in charge of making sure each chapter sent members.

This new change shook up Oregon a bit. A lot of guys had hitched their horses to Junior and gone against Lil Dave, Jeremy, and me. My only goal at the time was to reunite the state and get everyone back on the same page. The biggest thing was to make sure everyone supported each other and was brotherly, and that we cut out the drama and shit talking that undermined the brotherhood we worked so hard for. We started having a lot of region-wide, all-member meetings, and getting everyone to spend more time with other chapters in their region. For some, this was a welcome shift back to how Oregon had originally been, but there were some who didn't want to be active and spent more time bad-mouthing brothers than doing anything. They knew they would have to change or get on down the road.

Every year, the club holds a big national run and with it comes national elections. Junior, Peck, Roger Pinney, and other old-school members were working really hard behind the scenes trying to get those loyal to them to vote for the old-school and oust Lil Dave. These guys were all in leadership many years ago, and eventually most of them were thrown out under Doc as he changed the club. When Lil Dave became international president, he brought a lot of them back due to their history with the club. Some, like Junior, he even put back into leadership. But that turned out not to be enough for these guys; they were hell bent on being in charge again and "bringing things back to the old ways." Ahead of the elections, some Oregon chapters loyal to Junior saw the writing on the walls and two full chapters quit. A part of me was sad to see them go. I had brought most of them in over the years, and we'd shared some good times before politics and power changed the type of members they were. But the other part of me was happy to cut out the cancer and move forward in a more positive direction. At the end of the day, being a Mongol was about brotherhood, and guys like these were undermining that.

There were a lot of rumors and speculation as the elections approached, and the few that supported the old-school members were pretty quiet about it. The night before the all-members meeting and elections it became obvious who supported who. While 95 percent of the club was partying together at the event, a small faction was at Roger's house, planning their move. We took note of who was not in attendance at the event and moved their names up to the top of the list for the following meeting's chapter roll call. The next day the meeting started, and as I looked around the room, very few of the defectors were there. The doors were locked and the meeting began. Not long after, someone opened a back door and let these guys into the room. They ended up coming in from a door behind Mother chapter, maybe two dozen at most, most of them were old men– Roger had an oxygen tank. He made a number of demands and, because he didn't follow the proper channels and instead attempted a coup, his small group was met with violence. I won't get into the details, but it was wild, and I honestly don't think anyone expected it to go that way. Most of the defectors turned tail and ran. They left their "brothers" behind; some jumped over others to save themselves. It was an embarrassing sight. As the room was brought back to order, and all doors again shut, the Portland chapter of the Mongols, who had not traveled to the meeting with us and instead showed up with Roger and his crew, were left standing, beaten and confused. I quickly sat them down, hoping others didn't notice. As mad as I was at them, these were my brothers. I'd brought many of them into the club, and the patch on their backs said Oregon, so I did what I could to protect them. I placed them in the back of the room with security all around them during the rest of the meeting, and right before the meeting adjourned, I snuck them all out a side door and took them back to their rooms. Portland chapter had traveled down with the Vancouver, Washington chapter and some of them split rooms. But during the melee, Vancouver chapter left, not even going back to their rooms. Some went straight to the airport and some, in fear of the airport, drove back to Washington.

We spent the remaining evening protecting Portland chapter, which I later learned confused them. They couldn't figure out why I was helping them after all they had done, but they didn't understand that I cared more about the club and our state than I did about petty beef. When we got back to Oregon, all but one member of Portland chapter quit, and all of the Vancouver chapter quit, so I moved to Portland and helped restart it. The funny thing about all of this was, just like in Spokane, Junior put it all together, but he never showed up. In fact, Peck wasn't there either. It turned out that, during his time overseeing Utah, he was charging members extra money to join and was keeping the difference, profiting from each new member he brought into the club. When this came to light, he was put out in bad standing.

Junior brought a lot of issues to Oregon, but the one that was hardest to fix was drug use. Oregon always ran a stringent rule set and had rules against being drunk in public and another against the use of methamphetamines. Meth was Junior's drug of choice, and some of those more impressionable members who looked up to him ended up getting into it too. With him gone, the state was ready to rebuild and get back on track, which eventually we did. Portland chapter grew, we started new chapters in the state, and even opened a new clubhouse in Salem.

CHAPTER FOURTEEN

Breaking up with Amber had caused me to become more active in the club again. And talking about breaking up with Amber brings me back to my trip to Thailand, which I made in order to meet with the Mongols Australian chapter.

Back in the days of MySpace, when I was still a Vago, I was in contact with some guys in Australia who belonged to a club called The Finks. We stayed in touch on social media, and after one of their members went to prison after a shoot-out with the Hells Angels, they were looking for people to write to him, so I started doing that. I became close with The Finks in Australia and as they got banned–Australia has some pretty Draconian ways of dealing with motorcycle clubs and even being a Fink became illegal–they were thinking about joining other clubs. Because of our contacts, they reached out to the Mongols and we patched them over. The Mongols went from being a small club with only five members to being the biggest club in Australia. But it was getting them started and on the same page as us that caused me to make the trip to Thailand. As well as taking a hard line with motorcycle clubs, Australia has some pretty strict rules on who can enter the country, and my felony conviction meant I had no chance of getting a visa. Thailand is a popular holiday destination for Australians, so that's where we met.

(There's an old joke about entry to Australia, which I suspect Australians don't find funny. Someone lands at one of their international airports and presents himself at immigration. The immigration officer says, "Do you have any criminal convictions?" and the visitor says, "I didn't know it was still necessary." In fact, the answer "Yes" will get you put back on the next plane out, but the reference to how most of the original European migrants came to be there is one you can't ignore. Australia is where the British started sending their criminals after the War of Independence when the new United States of America refused to take any more.)

We called the trip to Thailand the Mongols' First World Run because we already had fairly new chapters in Malaysia, Bali, and Thailand, and this was a chance for us all to get together. This continued for me when I got back home because Lil Dave put me in charge of all the out-of-country chapters. What we wanted was to make sure that everyone was on the same page–that a chapter in Bali operated in exactly the same way as a chapter in California.

The second World Run was in Cabo in Mexico where we wanted to sit down with the Australians again to look at how things were organized. Someone who was a Mongol had been setting up chapters in Australia without approval, and we needed to check out how they were behaving. Nor was it just in Australia–for example, we found out there was a chapter in England with only four members, and they didn't go anywhere or do anything. They just wore patches and told people they were Mongols. One of them was actually an ex-Hells Angel, which was creating issues with the Outlaws. France and Denmark each had only one chapter, but Germany was pretty big, and Germany was really the only European country that seemed to want to run its operations in the approved Mongol way.

We couldn't have people calling themselves Mongols while taking no notice of the Mongol philosophy, so I sent out notices saying that we were going to close most of the European chapters outside Germany down. The Europeans, on the other hand, once again excluding Germany, had announced that they were going to have a European conference at which they would set up their own Mother chapter. In a sense, you could see their point–America had rebelled successfully against England and gone its own way, so why shouldn't people in Europe rebel against an American Mother chapter and go their own way too? Our attitude was very simple–they were very welcome to have motorcycle clubs operating anyway they chose. What they couldn't do was call those clubs Mongols.

The Danes wanted to stay in the club so we arranged that they would send a delegation to Mexico to meet with us, the Germans, and the Australians, but then things got a little crazy. It's usually very easy for Australians to get into Mexico, but the Australian government had reached out to the Mexican government and, when the Australians arrived, they were sent back home. So we ended up with just us, a German delegation, and a Danish delegation.

It worked out well. No one let the other European countries know that this meeting had taken place, and the Germans agreed to host the proposed European conference. Then, when people calling themselves Mongols from Italy, France, England, and elsewhere in Europe showed up, their patches were removed, and they were told they were no longer Mongols. The Germans sent all the patches to me, with photographs of the event.

I'd moved from Portland to Salem, where I was sharing a house with Nate, a guy I'd known since my punk rock days who had also become a Mongol. I was still going to graduate school, I was dating quite a lot (being single again), and trying to figure out what to do with my life. I got back into weightlifting.

Then I started a clothing line called Rain City Motor Culture (RCMC), which kept me pretty busy–and then I met Ashley. We had a couple of dates, we hit it off, and we started spending time together. I was still doing local club stuff, but as well as being focused on school, I was hanging out a lot with Ashley, and I was conscious that the club was becoming just that little less the center of my life.

And then I graduated. I had my master's degree. It felt pretty good. But, not long before I graduated, the program had required that I do two internships. My first was working with the homeless in downtown Portland. My second was to be a youth counselor with the Oregon Youth Authority, and this was close to my heart because I'd realized during my studies that working with young people was what I wanted to do. Everything went fine at first–I went to interviews and was hired as an intern at the Youth Authority. Of course, before I could start work, I had to be trained, and when I reached the address the Youth Authority had given me for the training, it turned out to be the Oregon State Police Academy.

I survived one day before they took me out of class and asked what I was doing there. They asked me to confirm that I was a Mongol, which I did. I told them I was planning to be a counselor, but they told the Youth Authority they didn't want a Mongol there in the Police Academy and the Youth Authority let me go, explicitly telling me that I was being fired because I was a Mongol.

I hired an attorney. I'd been fired because I was profiled–they told me that they thought my intention was to infiltrate, to start working in prison so that I could recruit kids for "my gang." Really? I went to school for eight years just so I could go into prisons and recruit kids who didn't even ride motorcycles? It was laughable. It was also illegal.

I won–the Authority settled. It was no great monetary value; I'd lost an internship, not a job. We agreed on $1001. But it wasn't the money that was important to me, it was the principle.

There was a downside. The case had been high profile, my photograph had been all over the papers, everyone knew I was graduating, everyone knew what I intended to do for a living. And there was spillover. At school, I'd been a wrestler; now I enrolled in a gym to train in Krav Maga, the Israeli martial art. I loved it, I wanted to do more, but the woman who owned the gym told me I couldn't train there. She had a lot of members who were cops, and they had said that they'd all leave if I was allowed in the gym. Why they would do that, I don't know. The only thing that makes any sense to me is they did it out of spite. Vindictiveness.

So I decided to train in jiujitsu instead. The guy who ran that gym had been on my wrestling team, and I reconnected with Brandon, who used to ride in a Christian motorcycle club that sometimes rode with the Mongols. I started going two or three times a day, five days a week.

I'd been in motorcycle clubs more than ten years, but now I was getting more and more into working out and jiujitsu, and less into the club, apart from which I graduated and was starting to look for a career. I began to think about maybe retiring in good standing from the club. My concern, though, was that if I tried to retire in Oregon, I would only be pulled back in because I'd started so much in that state. Ashley was getting ready to start graduate school herself in dietetics and nutrition. There was a program at Oregon State that she could attend. But then fate took a hand.

I was in LA, training for the Jiujitsu World Championships. I was pretty pleased with myself because I was beating pretty well everyone I came up against. I thought I must be really quite something. And then a team rolled in from southern Illinois. These weren't rich kids, they weren't well dressed, they didn't look much, but they kicked everyone's ass. The first one I took on beat me six times in one round. I thought this was awesome, and I spent the whole weekend with them. It reminded me of when I was in the band—these guys were like brothers. They trained together, ate together, did everything together. I wanted to be part of this.

I talked to Ashley. Southern Illinois University had a graduate program just like the one at Oregon State. What's more, my photograph had not been all over the Illinois papers. And there were no Mongols in Illinois, so I wouldn't be distracted by club issues. We decided we were going to move to Illinois. And it's worked out because we are still there, although, when I told Lil Dave I was going to resign, he told me not to do that. "Just be a Mother chapter nomad—you don't have to do anything, you can wear your patch while you ride, if that's what you want to do, and if you want to attend some other state's event, you can do it."

So 2017 ended up being the big year I was waiting for. I graduated with my master's degree, I won my lawsuit against the state of Oregon, I was awarded my blue belt in Brazilian jiujitsu from Professor Orlando Sanchez, and Ashley and I moved to southern Illinois to start a new chapter in our life.

CHAPTER FIFTEEN

W E DIDN'T HAVE A lot of stuff, but we did have three bulldogs. We put all three dogs in my car, everything else in Ashley's car, and drove to Mount Vernon, Illinois. It took us two and a half days to get there, and we were going somewhere we had never seen and knew almost nothing about. Mount Vernon is famous for having the only courthouse still in operation in which Abraham Lincoln argued a case. It isn't famous for much else, but Ashley and I found it a great place to live. It's a very small town, population less than fifteen thousand and my jiujitsu coach said places to rent would not be advertised–we needed to drive around and look for one. So we checked into a hotel while we drove the streets looking for a rental that would accept animals. We found one pretty quickly and we discovered one of the great advantages of moving from Salem to Mount Vernon–we'd been paying about $1100 a month rental and here it was $550. That brought a sense of freedom and contentment.

I got a job right away with the Community Resource Center, where I was doing traditional mental health counseling with a stress on youth counseling and counseling domestic violence perpetrators. This was my first job in the field, and the same sense of relief that I got when I discovered what rentals were like here came to me from the knowledge that I'd left Oregon and California behind. I didn't know anyone in Illinois and no one in Illinois knew me or anything about my past. That relief turned out to be misplaced.

I'd been in the job for about two months when I was sent for training on what was called the Meth Conference. This was a big conference where all the drug counselors in the state and the region got together to learn about new developments and new techniques. There were a lot of breakout sessions dealing with specific topics. Apart from that, the conference was an opportunity for professionals to meet, network, and swap information.

The conference was going pretty well and I saw that one of the breakout classes was on the subject of Outlaw Bikers. Naturally, I decided to check that out. There were no Mongols in Illinois, no one here knew who I was, and I wanted to hear what the specialists had to say. It turned out not to be true that no one here knew who I was. I sat at the back of the class and the guy in charge simply stared at me. Then he talked to his partner, closed his computer, and left. Another policeman came in and said, "Detective Green has been called out on a work emergency; there's no one else who can run the Outlaw Biker class, so we're going to talk about street gangs instead." And that's what happened, and I thought nothing of it. But halfway through the next class I was pulled out, and that's when I discovered that Detective Green was one of the head guys in the Outlaw Bikers Investigation Unit, which operated nationally and not just in Illinois. He was, of course, a good friend of Detective Burroughs, who had run the informant Odie in Oregon, got my parole revoked, and tried to get me additional prison time.

Why someone running a class on bikers wouldn't want a biker in there, I have no idea. But now Detective Green knew I was in town, and he did everything he possibly could to cause me trouble. He called the Community Resource Center and tried to get me fired, but it turned out that people in Illinois didn't just roll over on police instructions the way they had in Oregon. My boss asked me some questions, but he was cool about it. He didn't see why my being a biker should affect my work, and he didn't see it as a reason to fire me. Detective Green called a lot of other agencies that I worked with to warn them about me, and he visited the Mount Vernon Police Department and told them they should write me a ticket every time they saw me on my bike. Unfortunately for him, the Mount Vernon PD took the view that they had real crime to deal with, and they didn't have time to spare to make life difficult for some biker doing nothing but ride around town. In fact, they told me that they'd told him, "If he breaks the law, we'll arrest him. Otherwise, we're not going to mess with him."

Detective Green went to the gym where I did my jiujitsu training and tried to persuade them not to let me train there. He even checked out the social media accounts of cops who trained in the same gym and had friended me on social media and told them he'd get them fired if they didn't unfriend me. I probably should have been flattered by the amount of effort this man was prepared to put into knocking my life off the rails.

Before I moved to Illinois, I had been the one who did the sit-downs with the Outlaws when there were discussions to be had with them. There was a lot of overlap and mutual friendship between Outlaws and Mongols, and I got pretty tight with some of those dudes. At one point, I was doing a lot of sit-downs with their national president over European issues. The Outlaws started in Illinois and they were the only major club there, so I knew when I moved into the state they might have some territorial concerns. One of the first things I did was to contact the national president and let him know that I was here, I was here to work, my girlfriend was here to study, and I had no intention of setting up a chapter. He put me in touch with the state boss, we had the same conversation, and he was less friendly than the national boss, but he introduced me to Tug, the Outlaws' southern Illinois chapter head.

Tug called me and invited me to a birthday party. I didn't have a local chapter to check in with, so I let my brother and my coach know where I was going, and I went there and hung out with Tug and a whole bunch of Outlaws, after which Tug and I built a really good relationship, although the Mongol/Outlaw relationship elsewhere had its moments. I'd find myself sitting down with their national president in Indianapolis, in Florida, and elsewhere to discuss issues that had come up in those states.

With all of that going on, I came home one day to find that my bulldog, Lola, had had a spinal stroke. I took her to an emergency vet and then to some other vets, but she ended up paralyzed in her back legs. The surgery ran to about $12,000, which I didn't have, but I did a GoFundMe page and a lot of people from the club helped, a lot of my friends helped, and Lola enjoyed another three years of life before she passed away.

Oilpan, one of the Spokane Mongols, had told me that he was tight with guys from the hardcore scene in St Louis, they all rode motorcycles, and Oilpan suggested it wouldn't hurt to at least make friends with these guys. I was spending a lot of time with the jiujitsu team and Heath Pedigo, the head coach, was the brother of Randy Pedigo, who worked out of the same weightlifting gym I was at and was a noted hard man and MMA fighter. I met Randy soon after moving to Mount Vernon and Randy said, "If you ever start a chapter, I'd like to join." Randy and I started riding around together quite a lot. I followed Oilpan's suggestion and met the guys in St. Louis. They were part of a group called BDC, very into working out, one of them had a tattoo shop, they were keen on riding motorcycles, and we hit it off right away. We were hanging out every weekend, and eventually they said they wanted to be Mongols.

I was pretty well over it, but that didn't mean I wanted to stop other people, so I talked to Lil Dave, talked to the guys, and then I had to deal with the fact that I had told the Outlaws that we wouldn't start a chapter in Illinois. Most of these guys were from western Illinois, right up against the St. Louis border, so we agreed that we would have to make it a St. Louis chapter. We were the second chapter in Missouri, but the first big, main chapter. This opened up a whole bunch of issues, very like the ones I had been through in

Oregon. The main clubs in St. Louis were the El Forasteros and the Galloping Goose, both of which were aligned to at least some degree with the Hells Angels (some of whom were also in Illinois), and the Invaders, and none of them wanted the Mongols there. The Invaders were the first we sat down with, and we came to an agreement similar to the one I had come to earlier with the Gypsy Jokers: we weren't going to be friends, but we'd stay out of each other's way, we wouldn't go to each other's bars, and we wouldn't recruit each other's members. That relationship worked out okay.

The Hells Angels and the El Forasteros were trying to work out ways to keep us out and the Galloping Goose wanted to keep us out of Kansas City.

Lil Dave put me in charge of the whole Midwest and we went from having two members in Kansas City to a full chapter in Kansas City, a St. Louis chapter, and an Ozarks chapter. By the time I retired again, we also had four chapters in Indiana, one in Tennessee and– I'm afraid because I'd told the Outlaws I had no intention to do this, though I hadn't promised we never would–two chapters in Illinois.

The El Forasteros don't have the kind of structured leadership other clubs have. Instead, they have a board. This made it difficult because, although they were continually wanting to sit down with us and thrash things out (or that's what they said), reaching decisions was difficult for them. There'd always be someone who didn't agree with something and had the power to veto it. In the end, they got in touch with Lil Dave; one of their members from Iowa wanted to sit down and talk with him and me. Everything would be cordial. When I talked to the guy from Iowa to make the arrangements, he seemed cool, and we agreed that, to avoid any issues, we'd meet in a public bar in St. Louis. Somewhere we could be seen.

When the day came, he gave me the address where we were to meet and immediately it felt bad. The St. Louis guys said, "Hey, Mooch, that's not a bar. That's a warehouse those guys own." The message had said, "Go into the side gate, let yourselves in, we'll see you downstairs." So, a couple of hours before we were due to meet, I drove by in a car and in plainclothes to see what was going on. There was black plastic all over the windows and Hells Angels prospects in the parking lot. Not only did these guys think they were going to kidnap me, they also thought they were going to kidnap our national president. So we went to a bar a mile down the road, and I called them up. "We are not going to meet you there, but here's where we are and you're very welcome to join us here." And that was it; they didn't show and we never heard from them again. Lil Dave reached out to them and said, "Hey, that's not the game we're playing. If you guys want to meet and talk, let's do it," but there was no response.

We didn't really run into each other much after that. I heard that a bunch of El Forasteros were beaten up downtown one day and quite a lot of their members quit. They then did something unforgivable in motorcycle club terms–they decided that, if they couldn't drive the Mongols out, they'd get the FBI to do it. They went to the bars where their members had been beaten up, got the video footage, and sent it to the FBI. You just don't do that. The old guard in their club weren't happy with it, they told other clubs, and word got around fast.

It wasn't all hostile. We were still partying all the time with the Outlaws. They'd given us the key to their clubhouse so we could hang out there any time. Any event they held, we went too. We even talked about forming a national brotherhood between the Mongols and the Outlaws, to be called Black and White Nation.

It only took about a year for cracks to appear in the St. Louis chapter. One of the problems with bringing in a large group is that they were all friends before they joined, so if one starts to feel there's a problem, a lot of others will take his side. If one wants to quit, they'll probably all leave together. Although I tried to prevent it, there was so much drama following their departure from the chapter that they ended up leaving in bad standing. We still had enough members in St. Louis to carry on the chapter and I was able to keep it going.

As if all of that wasn't enough, I had some problems with my neck. This had actually begun back in Oregon, and I tried a number of chiropractors. I was told a cluster of nerves were balling up in my back. I had a lot of pain in my neck and down my arm and it was getting worse. It got so bad I wasn't sleeping, I wasn't training, and finally I gave up on the chiropractors and went to see a doctor. After an X-ray and MRI, a specialist in St. Louis told me I was suffering from OPLL, or ossification of the posterior longitudinal ligament. What happens is that the ligament running along the back of the vertebrae and disc hardens into bone. If you simply leave it, it can cause irreversible damage, so I was told I would have to have some of the vertebrae in my neck fused together. They also told me the surgery would have some effects on my life that I wouldn't like. I wouldn't be able to ride a motorcycle, and I certainly wouldn't be able to take part in jiujitsu. If I possibly could, I wanted to avoid that kind of surgery and I went to Indianapolis, Louisville, and Texas looking for alternative opinions, but they all said exactly the same thing. So, in 2018, I had major spinal surgery.

My whole neck was fused, my mobility was seriously altered, and I was in bed for three months. I still went to jiujitsu classes, and they built me a little bed in the corner so I could watch what was happening, but I couldn't take part. The jiujitsu team gave me all the help they could—they had cleaned the house for me before I came home and they looked after the dogs. Ashley took amazing care of me; she had to help me in and out of the shower and on and off the toilet. It was a hell of a thing to go through and I've no doubt it strengthened our relationship. And then, after four months, I was in physical therapy. I started walking around, I went back to work, and my recovery was going well. I hired a personal trainer and started doing a lot of kettlebell exercises and push-ups; I worked on my core strength and put back on the forty pounds I had lost.

I wasn't doing any live jiujitsu, but I did all the drills and then I did start jiujitsu with guys I really trusted–I couldn't have anyone pull my head or my neck because the risks were too great. I accepted that I was never going to be able to compete again. And I got back into riding. I'd sold my bike to a Mongol because I didn't think I'd ever need it again, and I still thought the best I would be able to do would be to ride around town, so I bought a cheap bike from a local dealer, but fairly soon I was riding to St. Louis, about fifty miles in each direction. And then in 2022, I rode all the way from Mount Vernon to Oregon and back. I ended up doing everything I'd been told I wouldn't be able to do, but it took a lot of work and a lot of support from Ashley, from the team, and from friends.

CHAPTER SIXTEEN

LOOKING BACK ON MY life, it seems I always had to learn from experience rather than learning from others. Unfortunately, especially when wearing club blinders, this cost me some of my best friends. Before I brought them into the club, Weedy, Oilpan, and I knew a lot of the same people, but I didn't know either of them. Nevertheless, we became close. Oilpan and I started by talking on social media. We grew up in the Northwest with similar backgrounds and a lot of shared experience. Spokane was more than five hours away from me, and we were trying to figure out some opportunities to meet up.

A bit before this, the NHRA Harley Drag Races were coming through Oregon, and the Mongols had decided to attend. As we often did, we met up beforehand and arrived in one big pack. We spent the day mingling with the other clubs and enjoying the races. The Bandidos are big into the race scene and a few of them were there from Washington. I had known of the Bandidos for many years but hadn't ever officially met any before this. We didn't end up talking at the event, but a few weeks later, I got a call from a Bandido nomad named Yankee. He had seen us at the drags, was impressed by how we carried ourselves, and invited us to spend the weekend with them at the Anacortes Oyster Run in northern Washington. This was a good opportunity to improve relationships with a national club that was also one of the biggest in the world, as well as get to know the ones in our region. So we agreed.

The Anacortes Oyster Run was one of their national runs, and I knew there would be several hundred of them there, so I didn't want to show up light. I made it mandatory for all Oregon and Washington Mongols and Raiders to attend. We rode up together, meeting up with the Washington members along the way. This was also my chance to meet Oilpan; he rode out with his father and uncle, and they joined the ride with us.

Initially, Yankee had suggested he meet us at the local Harley dealership and ride into the Bandidos' camp with us. They had their own campground, and he told us we could crash there. When we got to the Harley dealership, I called Yankee, but he was busy and just gave us directions to the campground. I had assumed he had let his club know we were coming, so we mounted up and headed to the campground. It was a bit off the road so the Bandidos could see us coming and were ready for us when we got there. As all forty to fifty of us pulled in in one large pack, I could see from the looks on their faces that they were puzzled. We were waved in, and as we pulled up and dismounted, we were quickly approached by the leadership and asked what we were doing there, which was how we found out Yankee hadn't told them we were coming.

Nevertheless, they treated us well, were super hospitable, and were incredible hosts. We spent the weekend hanging out, getting to know each other, and building relationships. As night fell and we were setting up out tents, I noticed more and more Bandidos were leaving. As it turned out, this area is notorious for rain; the Bandidos party at this campground, but most of them stay at local hotels. We were some of the few that stayed on the grounds and found out why so many did not when we woke next morning with several inches of water in our tents after a night of heavy thunderstorms.

Other than waking up soggy, it was a great event and became something the Oregon and Washington Mongols went to for a few more years after that. The campout was also a great opportunity to finally link up with Oilpan in person.

After that run, I started spending more time with both Oilpan and the Bandidos, eventually starting the Spokane chapter with Weedy, Oilpan, and a few others. Around the time Junior shut Spokane chapter down and I was moving to Whittier for school, Oilpan decided to move to Phoenix, Arizona, and Weedy moved to Los Angeles, so we still spent a lot of time together. Not long after I moved back to Oregon, Mother chapter agreed to restart Spokane chapter, and Oilpan moved back home to Spokane and got the chapter running again. Weedy had stayed in LA and was a member of Mother chapter for a while before joining Pico chapter. He had, in effect, been thrown out of Mother chapter and that would have consequences later. Oilpan was one of those who kept telling me I needed to check out jiujitsu. Both he and Weedy trained in it and they knew I would like it. Before I moved to Illinois, now that I had I gotten involved in jiujitsu and was focusing on graduate school and less on the club, I started to change how involved I was in the club. I had asked brother Menace, from Mother chapter, to step in and help out with the out of country chapters that remained after we'd shut a lot of them down. I had stepped down as the Northwest rep and suggested my brother, Jeremy, take over Oregon since he had been there with me from day one, and suggested Oilpan take over Washington. Lil Dave agreed and they both became state reps in my place.

We all stayed close even after I moved. I flew out to LA with the PSF team shortly after moving to Illinois to support them as they competed in the IBJJF No Gi World Championships. The team stayed at Professor Orlando Sanchez's gym, but I stayed in a nearby hotel. My neck pain was getting really bad by this time, and there was no way I could sleep on a gym mat. I was in serious pain that entire trip. While we were training at Orlando's, Weedy came out and met the team and trained with us. Pretty much anytime I trained in LA, Weedy would come out and train with me. He'd become one of my best friends over those years and we spoke often, if not daily.

Even after relocating to Illinois, the three of us remained very close. Oilpan had connected me with the St. Louis guys who initially became Mongols, and we all traveled to Spokane together in 2018 to support a run Spokane chapter was hosting. After introducing me to the STL guys, Oilpan also let me know he had a group of guys in west Texas that he had grown really close with. The St. Louis chapter and I were headed to Tulsa, Oklahoma for a club event, and I invited these Texas guys up to meet with me and the club.

Many years ago, when I was brand new to club life, even before I had gotten arrested for that big incident in Oregon, I was spending time at my friend Jade's tattoo shop in Portland. Jade had two friends from Australia visiting, a tattoo artist and a friend of both Jade and the tattoo artist by the name of Dave Bastard. We hit it off immediately. We spent a lot of time together and he even ended up buying a motorcycle from me. When Bastard returned to Australia, we stayed in touch, and he eventually joined the Mongols' first Australian chapter. This was before we patched over the Finks and there were only five Mongols in all of Australia. Bastard was the first Australian Mongol to visit the United States and attend a national run with us. While I was at the tattoo shop, I had met another artist who seemed a good dude, but I was focused on spending time with the Australians and didn't get to know him too well. A decade later, I was in Daytona with the new St. Louis chapter for Bike Week and this tattoo artist approached me and explained how we had first met at Jade's shop all those years ago, and how meeting us that day inspired him to become a Mongol. He had moved back to his home state of Oklahoma and was now a prospect for the Mongols. I was thrilled to have reconnected with him; I spent time with him in Daytona and stayed in touch after. Not long after that visit, he became a full patch member, and they called him Beast. Beast was also going to meet us at the Tulsa run. So we were all pretty excited. I was looking forward to introducing the St. Louis guys to the old-school Oklahoma members, to see Beast again, and to get to know the Texas guys Oilpan had sent.

When we got into Tulsa, we spent most of the day getting to know the Texas guys. They'd been introduced around and I was catching up with some other, older Oklahoma members when the whole vibe changed. Things got quiet, somber. And then it was announced our brother Beast had been run over by a drunk driver on his way to meet us at the event and had been killed. I felt like I had just been punched in the stomach. I was just telling everyone our story and how we had met so many years ago, and how excited I was to see him. The realization that he wasn't going to be there with a big hug and a smile hit me hard. We ended up leaving the event shortly after that and going straight back to St. Louis in silence through the night. We returned a week or two later to lay him to rest.

After I had graduated and was looking for jobs outside of Oregon, and while Ashley and I were trying to decide where we wanted to live, I flew to Florida and interviewed for a position just outside of Orlando. I also flew to Dallas for a job interview. I let the Bandidos know I was going to be in Dallas, and they gave me amazing treatment while I was there. They offered to loan me a bike to ride, rides to and from the airport, whatever I needed. I was staying with an old friend from high school and didn't need a bike, but I sincerely appreciated the offer. I got up early, found a jiujitsu gym not far from where I was staying, dropped in on an open mat, and had some tough rolls and met some great people. I also left with a massive black eye. If it happened again, I would choose to do the jiujitsu after the job interview, not before. And after the interview a lot of the Dallas Bandidos met up with me for dinner, and we spent several hours having drinks and getting to know each other. I was really starting to feel like I was getting close friendships within their club.

I met another Texas Bandido prior to my visit. I had met Jake via social media discussing an FXR that was for sale and moving on from bikes to life and just staying in touch. After we met, Jake was arrested and on trial for a big shoot-out where police killed several bikers in Waco, Texas. From what I gather, the government was trying to paint its usual picture of all 1 percenters as criminals. Jake's attorney was going to combat this by having 1 percenters from several national clubs testify as to their professions to show that being in a major motorcycle club does not mean you're inherently criminal. They had a lot of well-known club members on the list and the attorney called and asked if I would also be willing to testify. Mongols have a strict rule that no Mongol is ever to take the stand against anyone else, but in this case it wouldn't be against anyone; the goal was for me to testify about how long I had been in the club, what my professional degrees were, and what I did for a living. Lil Dave and Mother chapter gave their approval, and I let the attorney know I was willing to help. I never ended up being called, but the process brought Jake and me closer.

Since Oilpan knew I had some good relationships within the Bandidos, he wanted me to get a feel for whether it would be possible to start a Mongols chapter in west Texas, so I reached out to a few and just asked how it would go. Although they were all very cool and cordial about it, I didn't get the feeling it was going to happen. The Bandidos had been the only major club in Texas since their inception, and we didn't want to ruin a national friendship over one chapter. So we agreed to put it on the backburner for now.

Unknown to us, the Bandidos were going through some internal struggles, and during a national leadership change, several of the Hispanic members had stepped away from the club. Some of them reached out to the Mongols, went to California, and sat down with Mother chapter to discuss joining the Mongols. This was a big deal, and something that had the potential not just to change the relationship between the two clubs, but potentially put a lot of members' lives at risk. Because it was a big decision, Mother chapter spoke often about the pros and cons of the deal. Also, Lil Dave called and spoke to the majority of the state reps to get their opinion. I had spent years building a personal relationship with many members of the Bandidos, I didn't know any of the ones wanting to leave and join the Mongols, and I didn't think it worth doing, which is what I told Lil Dave. Oilpan was also against it.

I have always been a member who will express how I feel but, once the leadership makes a decision, I go with it. That's how these things work. And I had many talks with Lil Dave about the pros and cons, and when he decided they were going to do it, I said, "Let's do it." I won't get into it more than that, but what I will say is, as we had expected, it drastically changed the Mongols' relationship with the Bandidos. What made things worse for me was, since I was poking around about the west Texas chapter, many of the Bandidos I was friends with believed I had something to do with the statewide patch over, which I didn't. But as a loyal member, and loyal to my club's leadership, I followed suit and ended many long-term relationships with those in the Banditos that I had cared about.

During this time there were also a lot of major political moves within the Mongols. The club holds national elections every year. Elections were coming up and two other members were running against Lil Dave. No matter if it is on a national level or down to motorcycle clubs, or even unions or PTA, politics divide. When I had first joined the club, my mentor, the San Diego president who I looked up to the entire time I was a Mongol (and still do), had told me, "If you want to last in this club, stay out of the politics." And for years, I was great at that. But the longer I was in the club, the more vested interest I had in the areas and regions I had built, the support club I had helped turn into a national club, and the relationships I had made with other major clubs, the less staying quiet was the right thing for me. So I got involved in politics; I often attended national meetings and president meetings and was vocal about my stance on different topics. But, as I said before, once I was heard, whether I agreed with the decision or not, I went with it. I never held a grudge or went behind national leadership's back. Unfortunately there were others who were making their campaign against Lil Dave very personal. And Weedy was one of them.

CHAPTER SEVENTEEN

WEEDY HAD BEEN IN Mother chapter for a while and then moved to Pico chapter. Weedy would say he was kicked out of Mother chapter and, really, I'd have to say that was true. There was some stuff going on there and the result was that he held Lil Dave responsible for his ejection. Weedy hadn't been a national officer. As well as the leadership, Mother chapter also has members it regards as soldiers who are there for security and to protect the officers, and Weedy was a soldier. That still meant that he traveled with the officers, spent a lot of time with them, and was close with them so, whatever the issue was that caused the trouble (and I've never been told a version that I can completely accept), they transferred him to Pico. This sort of thing happens quite often, but Weedy took it personally. And that put me in a tough place. Weedy and Oilpan were two of my best friends, and I was a lot less tight with Lil Dave. We were close because of the amount of work we had to do together; he was the national boss and I was starting new chapters and doing sit-downs with other clubs, so of course there was a lot of contact between us, but it was purely a working relationship. I'd never been to his house, never been on his boat, didn't really know much about his life outside the Mongols.

I didn't want to be in the middle between Lil Dave on one side and Weedy on the other. I was trying to stay out of politics and especially out of negative politics. There were members who were running against Lil Dave in the national elections. There wasn't much chance they were going to win, but they were supported by people who were disillusioned with Dave and Weedy was one of those supporters. What worried me about that was that people who are very vocal in favor of losing candidates tend to find themselves out on a limb afterwards. And it did seem that Weedy was determined to make a big noise. I spent a lot of time talking to Weedy and Oilpan along the lines that having your opinions is fine and so is talking to your guys and voting the way you want to vote, but it's not a good idea to tell the whole world about it.

The elections were held. Lil Dave's opponents did not win. Oilpan wasn't happy, mostly because he was opposed to the Texas expansion, and Weedy wasn't happy because of his personal issues. Weedy showed up at a president's meeting with a list of things he said Lil Dave had done. There were a lot of illegal things on that list. If Lil Dave really had done them, Lil Dave had broken the law many times. We didn't know that while Weedy was reading out this list of crimes he said Dave had committed and money he said Dave had stolen, he had a Bluetooth device in his ear. We also didn't know his chapter was outside, down the road a little, armed and ready to come in to the president's meeting and intervene if Weedy was shown any violence. Now, I understand why Weedy might have felt concerned, but Mongols aren't allowed to do that. They are prohibited from fighting each other.

Weedy said what he wanted to say, and he was entitled to do that, but the way he said it was not good, and he was asked to leave the meeting. But then came the realization that he'd been in radio touch with a bunch of armed members while he was speaking. When they knew that, the whole room voted to put him and his chapter out of the Mongols in bad standing. That only created more problems for me. Being put out bad doesn't mean anyone is going to be out to get you, but it does mean there can be no contact between you and other members. Any Mongol found to have been in contact with someone put out in bad standing will incur the same punishment. If they discovered that I had continued communication with Weedy, I, too, would be put out in bad standing. And I regarded Weedy a good friend, and I didn't want communication with him to cease. I was on the phone a lot, both to Weedy and to Oilpan, trying to find some form of damage limitation.

To make things even worse, it was around this time that Weedy and Trinity, the girl whose entertainment company I had worked for, were getting married. Everyone knew they were getting married—it was going to be a big event and a lot of Mongols had been invited. Mother chapter put out a message saying that anyone who went to Weedy's wedding would be put out bad along with Weedy. Weedy was calling me regularly and asking whether I would be at the wedding. I said, "Listen, you're one of my best friends, we've been through a lot together, but you're asking me to choose between my friendship with you and the club. I've put all these years of my life into the club, we know the rules, we know what we are committing to when we get into it, and you just can't ask me to do that."

Weedy replied with a lot of cuss words and fuck yous and that was the end. We didn't speak again after that.

I reached out to Oilpan and I said, "Look, you do what you have to do, but you need to know if you go to this wedding you will be put out in bad standing. There will be no ifs and buts about it. And that applies not just to you but your whole chapter if they go." I wasn't the only person who gave Oilpan that message. Oilpan said he wouldn't go to the wedding, and every Spokane member I spoke to said the same thing. They didn't want to be put out bad; they wouldn't go. But they did go. Maybe Oilpan made the opposite decision to mine, that his friendship with Weedy was more important than being a Mongol. Maybe he thought that because he had become so important to the Mongols the ruling wouldn't apply to him. I don't know because I've never been able to discuss it with him, but he went and he took his chapter with him. It was a big wedding, a lot of photographs were taken, the photographs got back to Mother chapter and every

Mongol who had been there was put out bad. Including Oilpan and the whole of Spokane chapter. What I found particularly hard to bear was that they blamed me for it. Them being put out bad wasn't their fault and it wasn't Mother chapter's fault. It was my fault.

Workwise, I was fresh out of school and doing traditional mental health counseling. I enjoyed it. The way it worked was pretty much, "Come into my office, sit down, tell me what's going on," and try to find ways through what was troubling these clients. Talk therapy, in other words. I worked with adults and with children, men and women, but what I really enjoyed and where I thought I might be making a difference was in counseling perpetrators of domestic violence. Men who hit women, for the most part; there are cases that go the other way, where women hit men, but they are very much the minority.

Most of the people I dealt with were men who had been brought up or otherwise developed believing that it was all right for a man to hit a woman. They were sent to me by court order after hurting their spouse or partner or even their child. For the most part, they were there only because the court had told them they had to be and they really didn't think they had done anything wrong. What was sometimes amusing was that they'd come into the room, see me, assume that I was there for the same reason they were, and start talking to me as if I agreed with them. As if I, too, thought that women were there for men to hit.

That program produced a lot of positive change. Guys who, when they first came, would say there was nothing wrong with what they'd done by the end of their time in the program would be telling newcomers, "No, man, that's not okay, it's not cool, you don't do that."

I really enjoyed that part of the job, but I was also asked to do substance abuse counseling and I really didn't go for that. The problem with substance abuse, whether it's alcohol or drugs, is that there's nothing you can do until the substance abuser hits rock bottom and faces a simple choice: change or die. Like the domestic abuse clients, these people were sent by court order, but they didn't want to make a change. They listened to what I had to say, and they said whatever experience and other people told them we wanted to hear, but it was just role playing. They had no real intention of changing. Working with people like that—trying to change the habits of people who have no intention of changing—can be soul destroying. It's the kind of thing that gets you wondering why you bothered to come in in the morning.

On top of that, I had a caseload of more than a hundred clients and maintaining a personal connection was difficult when I had to look at notes to remind myself what we'd said last time. I was in danger of burning out. Then I was sent to aggression retraining therapy (ART), which included a lot of role plays designed to establish what kind of therapist each of us was. When that training was over, I was offered a number of positions. The one that most attracted me was from a local agency operating multisystemic therapy (MST), a way of working with young clients and their families to break the cycle of social disorder and prevent them falling out of school or out of their families. It takes a holistic approach to help young people on probation who are in danger of being kicked out of school and/or out of their families. The MST approach, instead of trying to fix the surface problem, aims to get at the problem's roots. What is causing this behavior? Why is this young person taking drugs/staying out of school/shoplifting? It's a great deal easier to help people not to do these things if you've done the work to find out why they started doing them in the first place.

For example, instead of saying, "This kid is misbehaving because of past trauma," which isn't actually very helpful, MST might say, "This kid is smoking weed because of inadequate supervision or a negative peer group or because of a lack of involvement in social activities (or a combination of those things)." It is, essentially, a way of asking, "What is driving this problem?" instead of the traditional approach of, "What's the problem and how is it internalized?" Then the interventions are based on solving the underlying problems and not on addressing how those underlying problems are outwardly expressed.

As soon as I got to know MST, I realized how well it resonated with me and my beliefs. I had to work with the kid but also with his or her social worker, teacher, coach, and parents. I quit what I was doing and moved over to MST in 2018, and it's still what I'm doing in 2023.

The national relationship with the Outlaws was still good. Outlaws were finding that having Mongols in their area helped them. We were riding together, hanging out together, partying together, and an old-school, well-respected Outlaw from Gary, Indiana got in touch with Tug, head of the Outlaws' southern Illinois chapter. He said the Outlaws were having a hard time in Indiana, their chapter wasn't growing, the Hells Angels were strong there, and they wouldn't mind having a Mongols chapter nearby. Tug put me in touch with him by phone. As it happened, there was a member from Reno who I knew fairly well who had moved out to Florida and was now working not far from Gary. I'd put him with another Indiana chapter because I didn't know what the national politics were in Gary, and I hadn't been in any rush to start a Mongols chapter there, but with the Outlaws' support, it wasn't long before we'd put together a fair-sized chapter, which we called Lake County chapter. It was on the east side of Chicago, but in Indiana.

It seemed, though, that every time we made progress with the Outlaws, we then took a big step backward. In Florida, an Outlaw shot a Mongol in the hand. It's a Mongol rule that if you mess with one Mongol, you mess with all of them. Mother chapter sent me to Indianapolis where I met a Mongol rep from Florida and another from the East Coast and we sat down with the Outlaws' national leadership. We worked all that out, things were going smoothly again, and then we had an issue in Nashville.

The Outlaws in my area wanted to be cool, the East Coast Outlaws wanted to be cool, the Outlaws in Indiana wanted to be cool, their national leadership wanted to be cool, but that isn't the way the Outlaws work. Each regional boss has a great deal of power and if any one of them thinks, "Fuck the Mongols, we don't care," then keeping things cool everywhere becomes really difficult. The Outlaws' old national boss, Harry "Taco" Bowman, one of the most well-known 1 percenters in the United States, who was in prison on two life sentences plus eighty-three years for organized crime and shooting, had just died on March 3, 2019. His funeral was a big deal, and I took some of the St. Louis guys with me. Every Outlaw in the country was there and there were thousands of them. The national Bandidos, with whom our relationship had folded, were there, but we ignored each other.

Although I'd talked with the state boss of the Outlaws, Grubby, this was the first time I'd met him, and Grubby had been upset for some time with the local Outlaws for talking to me because he said anything involving political decisions should go through him. He told me he was really upset about the Mongols setting up a chapter in Gary, Indiana and that I hadn't talked to him first. I explained that it was the Outlaws who had asked us to set up a chapter there and that we had previously not intended to do so. Faced with Grubby's anger, the Outlaw who had asked us to set up the chapter denied having done so. It was from that point that things began to go downhill.

The Outlaws threw Tug and a lot of his guys out of the club and appointed a new guy called Chris who was from Peoria, about four hours north of us. They said Tug's departure was because of drug use, and that's possible because he was becoming a heavy user, but there was an awful lot of politics involved. Jaybo was a member of Tug's chapter and there was no doubt he wanted to be leader.

Although Chris and I got on well, his political approach was more Chicago-based and the rules they ran by were different from what the Outlaws in our region had been used to. And Jaybo was also keen to stir the pot. I had gone to a bike night and Jaybo called Chris to say, "There's a Mongol here." So Chris called me and said,

"Where are you going to check in?" That is something that might, in fact, would apply somewhere like Chicago because there aren't any Mongols there, and if you are in the area and wearing a patch, you have to tell the Outlaws so. That's what is meant by checking in. We didn't have that agreement where we were, and by now I'd been there for a number of years. I made it clear, just as I did a few minutes later to Jaybo, that I'd never checked in before and I wasn't going to check in now, but Jaybo let it be known that from then on any Mongols wearing their patches in Illinois would have to check in. And we weren't going to do that. It was downhill all the way from there.

CHAPTER EIGHTEEN

Covid-19 meant that Ashley and I spent a lot of time together. We built a gym in our house, we were working out together, and we got really close. As things in the outside world returned to normal, we started going out together again, and we really got into hiking. We were in southern Illinois, we had the Garden of the Gods, and in fact, the whole of the Shawnee National Forest to get to know. We were very active.

Then a popular bar in downtown St. Louis put on a big Halloween event. Admission was by ticket, we knew it was going to be popular, and the number of tickets was limited, thanks to the aftermath of Covid. It was all to be over by 11:30 p.m., and Ashley and I decided to go. Junkyard Kenny, a local stunt rider and friend of ours who was becoming well-known nationally, came and so there were three people at our table, and then a couple of Mongols came in and joined us. Two or three more Mongols came in later. The evening was a sort of dance club party with everyone dressed up for Halloween. I wasn't drinking because I had to drive the seventy miles home later.

Ashley was dancing, we were all having a good time, and when 11:30 p.m. came and they kicked us out, we weren't ready to call it a night. Some of the girls from the jiujitsu gym texted to say they were at a bar in Mount Vernon so we made our way back there, and when we were close to home, we headed for the bar.

That may not have been the wisest thing to do, but you can't live your life always doing the wisest thing. This bar was the only one in

Mount Vernon that ever got crowded, but it was also probably the only bar in town that wasn't entirely safe. It was a place where, late at night, there were likely to be gangs, and there was likely to be trouble. I knew that before we went in, but it was Halloween, the girls from the gym were already there, Ashley was ready for more party time before she slept, and the bar was so close to home that I thought it was a chance for me to have a drink and party a little myself. A lot of guys from the gym had been providing the security there for quite a long time so I thought, *Okay, I know it's a bit of a dangerous place, but I'll know the people who are looking after things and everything will be all right.* That's not how it turned out.

We parked about a block away because it was crowded close to. When we got in, we found the bar had recently changed hands and the new owner had arranged new security. I didn't know any of them. The moment we were inside, Ashley said, "There's that guy. The one you have trouble with."

I don't want to name this man. A little under a year earlier, I had been at a wedding for someone from the gym and he had also been a guest. At the reception, he kept up a stream of negative comments on the wedding. "I don't know why everyone thinks this guy" (by which he meant the groom), "is so good at jiujitsu." "I don't know why everybody thinks this guy is so tough; I can kick his ass." He just kept running his mouth. I had with me a young guy from the jiujitsu team. He was just seventeen, but a really tough kid, and he wanted to fight the guy over the things he was saying. I didn't want a fight to ruin somebody's wedding, so I made sure it didn't happen, but this guy had got himself stuck in my mind. Strike one against him.

Then, during Covid, when the bars started to reopen after the lockdown, there was a bar that was able to open out back; they had an open patio and they could start letting people in before other bars. Ashley had a job as a bartender at the only five-star restaurant downtown and so knew a lot of people. And a lot of people knew her. So we were out one night and Ashley was on one side of the bar and I was on the other and this guy who'd run his mouth at the wedding was with a bunch of other guys and he shouted at Ashley, "Hey! Show me your tits."

Now, I am not possessive or controlling, and normally I'm happy to let Ashley look after herself, which she is very capable of doing. I half expected the guy to walk over and say, "Hey, I know Ashley from work, I was joking." I was ready not to make a big thing of it. And, sure enough, he walked over with a bunch of guys and I expected him to apologize. Instead of which, he stood there swaying, very drunk, and started poking me in the chest. "What are you on? What are you taking?" What he was asking was what steroids I was on. And now I was mad. First this guy yelled at my girlfriend to show her tits, and now he was poking me in the chest. So I looked over to his friends and I said, "You need to get this guy out of here." And they did that, and he left, so for me it wasn't a big deal. But that was strike two. I now knew who the guy was and I didn't like him, so when we got to this bar on Halloween and he was there, I said, "I'll just stay away from him."

So there we were, one other guy from our jiujitsu team and me with about twelve girls, dancing and having a good time, and eventually I needed to go to the bathroom. And when I came out, everyone had gone. Ashley told me, "That guy you don't like, he was grabbing all the girls. He grabbed one by the crotch, he was extremely inappropriate with another, and Ty (the other guy from the gym) got loud with him and we were all thrown out." Strike three.

I walked out of the bar and there was the guy I didn't like and all the bouncers standing in front of me. Ashley and all the girls in the gym were on the other side of the bouncers. The girls were telling the bouncers what had happened, but what we didn't know was that the head bouncer was Mr. Three Strikes's father-in-law. Ashley said, "That's right, he was grabbing the girls," and one of the bouncers said to her, "What do you know, whore?"

Well, enough is enough. I looked at the guy who'd been grabbing the girls and I hit him. Just once–that was all that was needed because I knocked him out. Now, I've been in a lot of bars and a lot of fights and I know what happens when you hit someone who is connected with the bouncers. So when the bouncers started to rush me, I stepped back, put my hands up, and said, "I know. I've gotta leave. I understand." I didn't want to go to jail, I wanted to keep the party going, somewhere else, obviously. I'd done what I needed to do and that's where I wanted to leave it. I told the girls and the guy from the gym, "Everyone get in the car. We'll meet up at the gym." And I made sure everyone did get in the car, which caused me a problem because I was parked a block away.

Ashley and I started walking away from the bar toward our car. And there was one really big bouncer, about six foot four, walking beside us. I didn't know it, but the owner of the bar had told the head bouncer, "That guy hit my son-in-law. Go get him." So this guy was pacing me, talking all the time, "Oh, you think you're so tough, you hit him with a sucker punch" and I was saying, "Yeah, man, whatever you say," because I really didn't want the police to arrive and take me in for questioning. I kept an arm out to make sure I kept him at arm's length, trying to deescalate the situation.

When we got to my car, the rest of the bouncers were there and I knew I was f****d. I'd sent everyone else away, and it was just me and Ashley. They formed a semicircle around me and my mistake was to take my eyes off the big guy who had been pacing me. It was Halloween, I knew not a lot of people would know who I was anyway, even if I hadn't been dressed like Hunter Thompson, and they would think they could get away with this with no repercussions. All I wanted to do was get me and Ashley into the car but they were blocking the way. And the head bouncer was giving me all this stuff about, "You fucked up, you can never come back here," and I was saying, "Yes, man, I know that," but as I looked at the head bouncer, the great big bouncer who'd been walking beside me punched me in the face hard enough that it put me on my ass.

This was only about a year since my spine had been fused and the effect of that fusion is that, when I get hit, my neck does not recoil. As soon as I hit my ass, all the background experience of my youth took over and I jumped up ready for a fight. But I put my hand to my chin and there was blood. So now I was thinking, *Great, he's knocked a tooth out, I'm going to have to go to the dentist, more expense.* And they were all backing away. They'd done what the bar owner had told them to do and they didn't want any more. So I said to be bouncer, "You fucked up, this isn't over, I'll catch you later."

We drove to the gym and I was trying to cool down; it worked for a while, but then I started to feel rough. I was throwing up and I was pissed because of (as I thought) the tooth I'd lost. I called Randy, one of the Mongols in town, and Randy came and checked me out, and then he and Ty gave me a lift home. When I got home, I was feeling even worse. I'd been drinking, so I thought that was the problem, but I had to face up to the fact that I was throwing up, and what I was throwing up was blood. I was in shock, not thinking clearly, and when Ashley kept telling me I needed to go to hospital, I would say, "No, no, everything is going to be fine." She helped me get into bed and I fell asleep. But when I woke, I was in the worst pain I've ever known.

What had happened was that when the bouncer punched me, he did not knock a tooth out, he split my jawbone right down the middle. The jaw bone was protruding through my gums and poking my tongue. I was in terrible pain, crying with it, and trying to work out what to do because, if I went to hospital, I'd have to say I'd been in a fight, and who would they report that to? I called my brother for his advice, but I could barely talk and all he could hear was mumbling, and he said, "Jeez, go to hospital and don't be a fucking idiot."

Ashley drove me there. It was less than five miles, but to me it felt like five hours. Before he X-rayed me, the doctor gave me dilaudid to ease the pain, which made me feel a hell of a lot better. When he had the X-rays he said, "It really is broken; you need immediate surgery, but there's only one plastic surgeon in this town, and he isn't available right now so you're going to have to go to Evansville." They told Ashley, "It will take about eighty minutes to get to Evansville, the surgeon there will wire his jaw shut, he'll be in surgery for about two hours, and you can go in the morning and pick him up." So after an argument, because she wanted to go with me, Ashley went back home, and I went in the ambulance.

As I said, it was less than a year since I'd had surgery to fuse my neck, so I thought I understood surgery. I remember when the spinal surgery was done looking at the clock before I was put under and looking at it again when I came out and thinking, "Look at that. You've been in surgery for four hours." Yes sirree Bob, I knew all about surgery. When we got to the hospital in Evansville, they told me they were going to put a plate in my jaw and then wire my jaw shut. "A couple of hours and you'll be in recovery."

By the time they put me under, it was 7:00 a.m. When I woke up, I looked at the clock and it was 3:00 a.m. And the clock had gone round more than once, though I didn't know that yet. What had happened was that, when they put me under, I had aspirated and my lungs had filled with blood. They'd had to force me into a coma, put a tube down my throat, and intubate me. I was actually in ICU for three days. Ashley, of course, had freaked out, and I do have to say that something that had started out looking like a straightforward procedure had turned into a hell of a big deal.

There was one consolation. My nose had been broken several times in a combative life, which meant I couldn't breathe through it very well, and so they had decided that I would have to go on breathing through my mouth, and they didn't wire my jaw shut. When Ashley got me home, Ty and one of the girls from the gym who'd been at the Halloween party had broken into our house. They'd filled it with Jello and soups and all that sort of stuff you eat when you jaw is wired shut.

Recovery took a while, and it was made more difficult because trouble with the Outlaws had started to grow. We were getting ready to set up a southern Illinois Mongols chapter. I'd been telling local Outlaws that this was something I was working on, and they were fine with it, but one of the things that was troubling us was how weak we would look if we didn't do anything about the Halloween night attack on me. In that world, you just can't let that happen. Someone does something like those bouncers did, and there have to be repercussions. And the repercussions have to be visible.

While I was still in hospital, all the brothers were calling and wanting to know, What can we do? What are we *going* to do? And by this time, the bouncers and the owner of the bar, as well as the guy with three strikes against him, would know who they had hit. We couldn't leave it.

And no one expected us to. One brother, I won't name him, but he had been a fireman and he'd left to concentrate on being in a motorcycle club, rode from Florida to Mount Vernon overnight, and by the time I got out of hospital, he had a complete list of everyone who'd been involved, their names, addresses, and work schedules.

I knew what needed to happen, and what needed to happen was that what we did should be public. If one of the people involved walked out of his home one day, fell down, and hurt himself, people might know about it, and they might connect it with the attack on me, but they might not. That wouldn't do. On the other hand, I didn't want me or any other Mongol to go to jail for what we were going to do. All my time in Mongol leadership I thought about what was low risk and high impact. We had to make a statement because I didn't want Outlaws or any other club to think anyone could attack a Mongol with impunity, but I didn't want any Mongol going to prison for it. People in town had to say, "Oh, yes, we know this happened, and THIS happened in return."

A week after I got out of the hospital, I had a big group of guys in plainclothes and driving cars rather than motorcycles park close to the bar where the problem had started. When the bar started to close at 2:00 a.m. and everyone was leaving, so that the bouncers and the bar staff could clean-up, these guys pulled up their masks and started to walk in. The bouncers slammed the doors shut, nobody got hurt, but it was very visible, and everyone knew it had happened. They also knew why; the bar staff were telling each other, "Get in the cooler, they're not here for us." The bouncer who had hit me ran out the back door. Word got around, "Stay away from that bar."

A couple of weeks later, a bunch of Hispanic Mongols came down from Chicago and Seattle. Mount Vernon is largely white or black; there aren't many Hispanic people there. These visitors went into the bar, two at a time, and in plainclothes so as not to draw attention to themselves until there were about fourteen of them in there, standing around in the corners and by the exits. They stayed quiet—when a bartender asked them if they wanted a drink they didn't say a word—and it didn't take long before security realized why they were there. Including the guy who had hit me. He was asking for help, and the others were making it clear that it was his problem. They got scared and called the cops, and the cops did a walk-through and said, "It's a bar, it's open to the public, they're not doing anything, there's nothing we can do about it." When the cops had gone, one of the Mongols touched his hat, and all of them stood up, making it clear for the first time that they were one group. They walked outside and stood there, staring through the window at the guy who had hit me. He left his job, just didn't show up ever again. All the other bouncers quit, and I felt that was a win for me. The guy who had hit me called and apologized; the head bouncer called and apologized; we had gotten our message across without anyone being hurt or any of our people risking prison.

All of that happened in October. In the previous August, there had been a big biker event in Indiana called the Boogie. There were bands, a big wet T-shirt contest, all the usual biker stuff you see on TV. It isn't something I'm super into, but a bunch of Mongols were going, so we decided to check it out. We met up at the local Harley Davidson dealership in Mount Vernon. There were two guys in the dealership who were in good shape; they obviously worked out. I was interested in whether they were local because of my plans to build a southern Illinois chapter. Before I approached them, I asked the salesman about them. "Are they from around here?" Yes, they were, and they were brothers. "They look in good shape; are they cops?" No, they weren't; one worked on the railroad and the other was a coal miner.

So I introduced myself to them and we talked, and one of them, Mike, said he wanted to get into jiujitsu. The other brother was Marc. We talked for a bit and swapped phone numbers, and then the Mongols and I left for the Boogie. Marc and Mike were the two guys who eventually helped me start the southern Illinois Mongol chapter.

The reason I'm talking about the Boogie was a guy called Dealer Dan who had been a Mongol for about fifty years. Dan kept calling me. "I've got these guys over here. I've got those guys over there." And I liked Dealer Dan, but a lot of the people he was sending me were not the kind I would usually hang out with. Nothing wrong with them, but they weren't our style, and they weren't a good fit with the Mongols. He wanted to start a chapter at the Lake of the Ozarks and I kept putting him off because these just were not the right people and it wasn't something I thought we should be doing right then. But Dan arranged for these guys to come to the Boogie to meet me, and I had to accept that I'd been wrong about them. There were good guys. A youngish guy called Blane had been in the army, he was into jiujitsu and MMA, used to race motocross, and we clicked right away. I also got tight with a couple of Indiana prospects who'd been put on guard duty, and their job was to make sure I had everything I needed and didn't get into any trouble. The end result was that I decided to give these guys a chance and start a chapter there.

It wasn't something I could do straightaway, so I went back to the Raider program. I said, "You guys are at least three hours from the nearest Mongol chapter, so you can't be prospects and get patched that way. Why don't we start you as Raiders, give it a year, and if at the end of that, you haven't had a lot of trouble with the local clubs and everything else is working out, I'll consider patching you over to the Mongols." And that's what we did.

CHAPTER NINETEEN

THERE IS SOMETHING ABOUT being a twin. Perhaps having someone with you literally since birth drives a desire to always have someone near you to share your life with. Pretty much as far back as I can remember, I have always had a girlfriend. The therapist in me will attribute that to some form of codependency, as well as to the culture of the era in which I grew up. I met my first girlfriend, Rae Adams, in the third grade so I use the term "girlfriend" loosely. We went on chaperoned dates to Mc Donald's, and later, a youth dance club her family owned. She would attend some of my sporting events, and in the fifth or sixth grade, we held hands one night at a little league game. Then came junior high, and I had moved schools. Charity Hubbard was my first kiss, in the seventh grade. Then there was Sarah, and a few others. In grade school and most of junior high, I was a jock, into sports, so I set my sights on the preppy girls. But going into high school as a punk rocker, and later skinhead, made me less popular with the preppy crowd, and I dated within my little subculture. I had a punk rock girlfriend my freshman year, Jenny, and then Nicole. I was still wrestling, but skipped practice a lot to spend time with Jenny. Then came Christal. I was a junior and she was a freshman. She was from a well-off family, her dad was an ex-cop, she was Italian, which my grandpa liked, and she was not a punk rock girl at all. She was the first "normal" girl I dated in high school. And I was a bad influence. Her parents would drop her off at Bible study after school, and I would be waiting down the street to pick her up and hangout with her. I spent the rest of high school dating Jessica. After I graduated, I had to turn myself into jail to serve thirty days for my assault charge. I was in a work dorm and allowed visitors. The dorm had windows onto the parking lot, so any time a woman came in to visit, all of the inmates would check her out. I had a good number of visitors. Julie (a high school crush who I never dated), Kristen, a high school cheerleader who I used to have a crush on in school (not the one I later dated), and Jessica all came to visit often, and the inmates were pretty impressed.

Jessica and I moved to Portland together once I was released from jail and lived together for a bit. Then there was Tawny, who I worked with at Hot Topic. Although close to the same age, Tawny was much more mature than me. She worked in the music industry and toured and worked with other bands. I was jealous and immature, and it didn't work out. When she left one summer for Ozzfest, I had a hard time with her being away, and she eventually broke up with me. I dated a bit and then met Kristin who I was with, on and off, for over five years. After Kristin and I finally called it quits, I was in and out of jail pretty often, moved to San Diego, and back to Oregon. I dated casually, but nothing too serious until I met Shawnta. Shawnta and I dated for a couple years and even moved in together. But not long after we started living together, I realized this wasn't going to be long-term, and I moved back with my parents while I looked for a new place to live. Shawnta and I were not broken up long when I met Amber. I actually knew Amber in high school as she was Christal's best friend. Amber was also a twin. Way too often when people found out I was dating a twin they would ask if my brother was dating her sister. Amber was very different than the girls I had been dating. She was religious, family oriented, and naïve to the type of lifestyle I had been living. However, she was open to dating a tattooed biker, and we spent a lot of time together. Amber ended up moving with me to Los Angeles, and when we moved back to Oregon, we had a few places together, first in Woodburn and then in

Portland. Amber was a special education instructor and was going back to school, working on her master's degree, and supported me sticking with school and working toward my own master's degree. Although things weren't perfect, they often seemed like it. After four years together, I ended up proposing to her, and we spent the next year planning our wedding. Growing up in Oregon with a lot of friends, being in the Mongols for almost a decade at this point, and having a large Italian family, we were planning a big wedding. We had gone to Hawaii together one year and really enjoyed it and were planning to return for our honeymoon. Amber often helped me keep my bad habits in check. When we were visiting Maui, the Hells Angels had recently started a chapter there, and we saw a few prospects in passing on the road. One night leaving a luau, and definitely after too much to drink, a local Hells Angels prospect was riding up and down the main street, going about five miles an hour and revving his motor for attention. I had this great idea and picked up a coconut and planned to hurl it at him and knock him off his bike. I thought it was a great plan, but Amber talked me out of it, which was probably for the best. I wasn't in the proper state of mind to be fighting with the locals.

We often argued about the wedding planning. It was going to be expensive, and her top priority was saving for the wedding. I was working at a motorcycle shop at the time while being a full-time student, so not only was I not making a lot of money, but I was often spending the money I did make on motorcycles and motorcycle parts. This did not go over well. Things were getting pretty rocky as I planned a trip to Thailand for the Mongols first World Run. I had invited her to come with me, and she said she couldn't make it. That was pretty much the last time I saw her in person. She left me by text message, and I returned from Thailand to an empty apartment. As I said before, a lot of the issue was due to me not wanting children, and her wanting a family, but at the end of the day, we were in different places in our lives and wanted different things.

I spent the next year single. It wasn't easy, and I really got into drinking and partying pretty hard. Then I started dating a lot. Nothing serious, but I was going out often. I knew at my age, newly single, I needed to get in shape and that motivated me to get back to lifting consistently, and I ended up putting on close to twenty pounds of muscle in the year after the breakup. As a therapist, one thing I often tell my clients is that you cannot truly be happy in a relationship until you can be happy alone. Once you are comfortable being alone, you will no longer ignore red flags or put up with things in a relationship that do not make you happy due to the fear of being alone. So many people stay in unhappy and even unhealthy relationships out of fear of being alone. I was getting comfortable with being alone. I was going on dates, but I was in no rush to get back into a relationship, and I definitely didn't want to get into one when I was still getting over the last one.

And, then, close to a year after Amber leaving, I met Ashley. Our paths had crossed when, after a day of riding, a group of Mongols unknowingly walked into a bar she was bartending at. She remembered us because we had all ordered Mountain Dew and no alcoholic drinks that day. Other than ordering my soda, we didn't talk that day. She later saw me on Facebook and sent me a friend's request. It was a few months later that I noticed her; she had liked a photo or post I had made and I remember thinking, *Who is this beautiful woman?* So I looked at her page and sent her a message to see if she would like to hangout sometime.

She took a few days to respond, which I now know was intentional. Then we went out on a first date. Ashley was adamant about making a good first impression and had told herself there wouldn't be so much as a kiss on this date. So, when the date was over and I walked her to her front door and leaned in for a good-bye hug, she preemptively lowered her head, thinking I may try and kiss her, and headbutted me right in the face. We started seeing each other a lot more often after that, and it didn't take long for things to get serious. I had told myself I was going to stay single for a few years, but Ashley's infectious laugh, beautiful smile, and incredible attitude had me rethinking all of that. After a few months of dating, I asked her to move in with me.

I was traveling a lot, doing club stuff, and in the past, I hadn't really taken Amber with me on club runs, but I was doing things different this time around and brought Ashley to a lot of events. Within the first year, we had traveled to Los Angeles, Florida, and Mexico together. As she has always done, from day one, she supported me during my lawsuit against the state. She had my back when I was kicked out of Krav Maga and in everything else that I did. She was my biggest supporter and always there for me when I needed her. She even supported me financially when I first graduated and the only jobs I could find in the field were parttime. Ashley had a design degree from the Fashion Institute of Design and Merchandising (FIDM), but she was looking into going back to school for a degree in dietetics and nutrition. She was enrolled to start at Oregon State University when I floated the idea of moving to southern Illinois. As luck would have it, Southern Illinois University offered both bachelors and graduate level programs for dietetics and nutrition, and Ashley agreed to a new adventure and moved across the country with me after only dating for about two years.

Dating Ashley, I quickly realized why my other relationships hadn't worked. It didn't take long for me to realize that this was the woman I wanted to spend the rest of my life with. I not only romantically loved her more than I have ever loved anyone, but she was also my very best friend and confidant. She was the first person I called with good news, the first person I went to when needing advice, and the one person I always wanted by my side. I loved everything about her and decided it was time I ask her to marry me. She and I had talked about marriage, and when on day dates in St. Louis, I would take her to jewelry stores and have her show me rings she liked. I planned a trip for us for her birthday in August

2020, a few weeks after the Indiana Boogie. I had invited some of our closest friends. She thought I was inviting them to celebrate her birthday, but they knew I was going to propose. And on her birthday, with our very closest friends, in front of the fountains at the Bellagio casino, I got down on one knee and proposed to her, and she said yes!

Vegas was an incredible vacation and a nice break from all of the drama that was going on back home with the increasing tension with the Outlaws and issues we were having at the Lake of the Ozarks. But time waits for no one, and soon I had to get back home and back to it.

CHAPTER TWENTY

THE TWO MAIN ACTORS in the formation of the Lake of the Ozarks Raiders were Frank and Blane, father and son. They had both grown up in the area, and they had some issues with a guy called Tonka who was a member of the Galloping Goose motorcycle club, which was aligned with the El Forasteros. We as Mongols had previously had issues with the El Forasteros in St. Louis, culminating in an attempt to get me and Lil Dave to meet them in a warehouse where it's safe to say they had planned at the very least to kidnap us. Whether we'd eventually have gotten out with our lives I don't know because they didn't tell us what their plans were. In any case, we called them and proposed a different venue, at which point they abandoned the idea of a meeting.

A lot of people in the motorcycle club world seem to want a title. Post *Sons of Anarchy* everyone wants a patch on their chest that reads, "President" but most do not understand the work and the risks that go with that position. I first joined the Mongols Motorcycle Club during an era of massive expansion. The southern California club was opening chapters all over the United States and even in other countries. The attitude of the leadership at the time was, "We are Mongols, we don't ask permission, and we go where we want!" As my experience in the club world grew, I realized this was not always the best way to go. I had helped start chapters of the Mongols all over Northwest and Midwest America, and even helped get the Mongols into Australia. What I found worked best was open communication with the existing clubs in the area when possible. The Galloping Goose ended up being one of those clubs with which diplomacy did not work.

The Galloping Goose were never slow to produce a slogan; "There'll never be Mongols at the Lake of the Ozarks" was one they came up with now. That was, of course, a red rag to a bull because while, on the one hand, my policy has always been to coexist if at all possible, it also says that no one tells the Mongols where they can and can't go.

Frank and his wife were out at a restaurant for breakfast when Tonka and two of the Galloping Goose jumped him in the parking lot. That didn't work out too well for them because Frank took a gun from one of them, and he was the one who came out on top, but that was the sort of thing that started when we set up the Lake of the Ozarks Raiders.

Earlier that year, we were still hanging out with the local Outlaws. We told them about the proposed south Illinois chapter and they were cool with it. They told us about a motorcycle rally put on in September every year at the Lake of the Ozarks by the Galloping Goose and said that this year they were going to it. As the Galloping Goose had said there would never be Mongols at the Lake of the Ozarks, it was obviously an excellent opportunity for us to get as many Mongols there as possible. The local Outlaws gave us details of the hotels they planned to stay at, and I spent the summer arranging to get as many Mongols as possible to go on the Lake of the Ozarks run.

Then Outlaws leadership took a hand and Grubby, the Outlaws state boss, told our local Outlaws not to go on the run. Grubby did that a lot; he would find out that the Outlaws were talking to me and he would intervene to stop things happening.

The absence of the Outlaws meant that their hotels were free, which was just as well because we had more than two hundred Mongols on the Lake of the Ozarks run. They were there from

Oregon, from Colorado, from out East–180 motorcycles and more than 200 Mongols in this little lakeside town. We intended it to be a big demonstration that we weren't going to be told where we could go, and that's how it turned out. We were there for the weekend and there was no trouble. The Galloping Goose and the El Forasteros held a party, and we rode by it in convoy, just to let them know we were there.

After that had all passed off without trouble, someone claiming to be a Galloping Goose was sending text messages to one of the Mongols in Kansas City so we took a bunch of Mongols in plainclothes up to Kansas City to look for him. We didn't find him in any of the Galloping Goose bars, so we went to their clubhouse, but they said they knew nothing about him. After this incident, we came to an agreement with the Galloping Goose that we would just ignore each other.

Overall, things were going along okay, but it was getting a little tense. I'd been talking quite a lot to Chris, who had taken over running the southern Illinois Outlaws chapter after Tug, and I told him we planned to start a southern Illinois Mongols chapter. He was cool about it, but he said, "I don't think Grubby is going to like it." One of my negotiating points was that I knew the Outlaws didn't want us in Chicago because Chicago was where the Outlaws had started. They'd fought a bloody war to keep the Hells Angels out of Chicago, and they didn't look kindly on the idea of any other club forming a chapter there. Their fear was that, if they let us form a southern Illinois chapter, a Chicago chapter would be next, and I had told them that I had no thought of forming a chapter in Chicago. Lil Dave and Mother Chapter had assured me that they had no plans for a Chicago chapter either. There were half a dozen Mongols living in Chicago, but they belonged to the Lake County chapter in Indiana, just across the border.

Still, although our relationship with the local Outlaws remained good, it was deteriorating elsewhere. Jaybo down in Marion made trouble whenever he could; he demanded that Mongols visiting

Marion check in, and checking in was not something we were going to do. That was part of our policy that we didn't look for trouble, but nobody told us where we could and couldn't go. That started the question: If we were going to have to put up with this shit, why were we troubling to ask permission?

Lil Dave gave me the green light to start the southern Illinois chapter. I reached out to the Outlaws to let them know what we were doing. Chris was trying to get me to sit down with Grubby, and he said it would happen at a restaurant, which would favor neither of us, but then they scheduled it in their clubhouse. I wasn't going to sit in their clubhouse and be told behind their doors what we could and couldn't do. And now the situation was complicated by what was happening elsewhere because relations elsewhere between the Mongols and the Outlaws were not as cordial as in Illinois. As a result, Lil Dave decided that we should meet their national lack of cooperation with a lack of cooperation of our own and set up a Chicago chapter.

This put me on the spot because I'd been saying for years that we didn't intend to do that. I didn't want to do it, but that isn't how club leadership works. If the boss tells you to do something, you do it. And Lil Dave told me to start a chapter in Chicago.

That was the end of all communication between me, Grubby, and Chris. I was still talking to the Outlaws' national president and he was trying to figure out ways to make it work, but Chicago wasn't having it.

One of the Mongols who lived in Chicago, but was attached to an Indiana chapter, had been to a chapter meeting, and on his way back, he stopped in a Chicago bar, still wearing his Mongols patch with an Indiana rocker. An Outlaw in the bar told him he wasn't allowed to wear the patch in Chicago and punched him in the face. You don't lay hands on a Mongol. We don't stand for it. Nor do you tell us where we can and can't go. We couldn't get any sense out of Grubby, according to whom it just hadn't happened, so we told the

Outlaws we were launching both Illinois chapters—one in the south and one in Chicago—and all communication with them ceased. There'd been a good relationship between Mongols and Outlaws for twenty years; I personally had been friends with them for more than ten years; it was all over.

And that was how 2020 ended. I expected 2021 to be a pretty wild year. Just how wild it would turn out to be, I had no idea. Early in the year, an old southern Illinois Outlaws member, Ego, asked for a meeting, and I arranged to meet him in the Marion Harley dealership. He knew he was on his way out of the Outlaws for the second time and wanted to talk about moving to the Mongols. That would have broken an agreement we had with the Outlaws that we wouldn't take any of their ex-members. Worse, Ego's problems with the Outlaws were caused by his drug use, and I didn't want to see heavy drug users becoming Mongols. So I said no. He couldn't be a Mongol. Someone else who wanted to be a Mongol was Tug, who had been the Outlaws' southern Illinois leader before he was expelled. I loved Tug and I thought he'd be a great Mongol, but we couldn't take him because it would have broken our agreement.

Instead, I told Ego and Tug the Pagans were expanding and taking members from lots of clubs. I had a friend who was in charge of recruitment for the Pagans and I put them both in touch with him. They both joined the Pagans in mid-2021, but Tug was not a Pagan for long before he was gunned down in his prospect's front yard.

Whoever killed him has not so far been caught, but Jaybo was heard to say that the Outlaws were responsible. Then law enforcement told me that they had been told the Outlaws also had a hit out on me. I don't know whether that was really true. Jaybo was running his mouth a lot and saying, for example, "We got rid of Tug and Mooch is next." I have no way of knowing whether he was speaking just for himself or for the Outlaws. Nevertheless, I took it seriously. Just to make sure that relations with the Outlaws were even worse, a bunch of Outlaws beat up Ego and took his phone. The phone was not password protected so they were able to read all the messages that had passed between him and me when I told him he couldn't be a Mongol, but he should join the Pagans and I would help him.

We honored Tug's death with a joint ride for Mongols and Pagans in Marion, and a Mongols ride in Chicago. In the Chicago ride, a bunch of Outlaws in plainclothes and in cars and not on motorcycles attacked Mongols. The Mongols were prepared for it; a couple of Outlaws were run over, a couple were stabbed, and at least one was shot so it didn't work out well for the Outlaws, but it was a clear signal that that was the end of our relationship.

Something we'd always made clear was that we'd continue to honor our agreement because we didn't feel we were responsible for any issues there might be, but if anyone laid hands on a single Mongol, then all bets would be off. A month after their attack, we were in Daytona once again for bike week. The Outlaws had asked for a standdown during that week. Lil Dave had suggested to their national president, "Why don't we meet–just you and me–and settle this between us?" but the Outlaws' president had refused the invitation. Just to demonstrate that the attack meant we were no longer obliged to stick to any agreements, while in Daytona, we set up a Mongols Miami chapter that included a number of ex-Outlaws. One of them was the one who'd ridden all the way to Mount Vernon to support me after I'd had my jaw broken.

*   *   *

I saw a cartoon once that summed up the way life sometimes lulls you into a false sense of security. A man was walking down the street, his head held high, a smile on his face. He was whistling. He had a smile for everyone. And behind him, invisible but implacable, a huge hand curled so that the first finger was held back by the thumb. At any moment, whoever owned that hand (Fate? God? Dame Fortune?

Take your pick) could release the first finger and send the whistling man to his doom. I felt I had my life under control. I was living with the woman I knew was right for me; I had my master's degree; I was being paid to do a job I loved and knew I was good at; Ashley and I had the dogs; and I was a respected member of what, for me, was without question the world's best motorcycle club. Life seemed as close to perfect as it could get. Most of those things I would hold onto, but the day was coming when I would no longer be a Mongol.

I said earlier that, although I'd known Lil Dave for years, we'd never been close friends. I hadn't, for example, ever been invited to his house. That changed with the number of times we met to talk about expansion in the Midwest and our issues with other clubs. Then, in May, Dave's wife, Annie, invited Ashley and me out to Los Angeles for Lil Dave's birthday party. Dave and Annie were known for throwing big themed parties and this year the theme was Studio 54. They had rented out a place that was made to look like Studio 54 and all the guests wore disco clothes. It was an incredible party and proved to me that Dave and I were becoming close friends outside of the club. I remember sitting down with Dave on that trip and explaining to him, in detail, the guilt I felt about Tug because I felt I had helped lead him down that road. We talked a lot that trip, and I felt good knowing I had Dave's support and love.

Shortly after that, Oregon lost its very first Mongols. Mongol TNT was the first Oregon member to join chapter thirteen. After a nice evening ride with his wife, on the way home from a night out, TNT lost control of his bike, and he and his wife died together in a motorcycle accident. Coming so soon after the death of Tug, this hit me hard. I flew out to Oregon, borrowed a bike from a close brother, and spent the weekend grieving with the brothers and celebrating TNT's life. Eugene chapter of the Mongols had been a chapter for just over thirteen years at this time, and TNT was the very first member in all of Oregon to pass away during that time. As a founder of the Oregon Mongols, and someone who helped bring

TNT into the club, I had to make sure I was there in Oregon with my brothers.

During my trip to LA for Dave's birthday, Dave had asked what Jeremy and I were doing for our fortieth. I told him we didn't have anything planned and often didn't do much more than go out locally for dinner. Dave and his wife, Annie, decided to throw a fortieth birthday party for both of us at the Mongols Mother chapter clubhouse in Downtown LA. It was, hands down, the biggest and best birthday party I have ever had. There were hundreds of Mongols there, and Annie went overboard with incredible decorations. With all of the death, threats of violence, and drama going on back in the Midwest, this reminded me why I was a Mongol and what the patch meant to me. I felt so much love and appreciation that weekend. Members came from all over the Midwest, Oregon, and California to attend. Of course, my Miami brother was there as well. We had been spending a lot of time together since he became a member. And although I didn't know it at the time, this party would serve as the last time I would see my brother, Blane, and the last time I would see Lil Dave as a Mongol. I had this huge bash, felt so much love, and soon everything was about to come crashing down.

*   *   *

A year had passed for the Ozark Raiders, and because they were staying out of trouble, but being active, growing, and making a good presence at the lake, we patched the Raiders over to Mongols and officially started the Ozark Lake Mongols. Blane had been really good at keeping his guys out of trouble and still remaining active and riding all over the lake, attending events like bike nights. Mid-afternoon one Thursday, they were at a bike night in downtown Lake of the Ozarks, just a few doors from the bars we had visited during bike week the year before. While Blane and his chapter were inside the bar, several Galloping Goose and some of their friends went into the bar and surrounded them, pushed them around, and tried to get them to fight. Blane held his ground and calmed the situation. The Goose all ordered bottled beers and went and stood out front of the bar. Blane thought the best move would be to just leave and deal with the Goose another day. It was broad daylight at a very crowded bar in the middle of the week. Blane told his guys it was time to leave and they walked outside towards their bikes together. They had to push through the crowd of Goose to get to their bikes.

While Blane was turning his ignition switch, some of the Goose attacked guests of the Mongols in the back of the group as they were trying to leave. Blane, never one to leave anyone behind, went back into the crowd to help his friends and was shot multiple times. He died on the scene. As police arrived, the two clubs scattered, and the Mongols stayed there with their friend, their brother. The police put a blue tarp over his body and left him on the sidewalk while they worked on their investigation.

I was out to dinner with the southern Illinois chapter when Blane's dad (also a member of the Ozark Lake chapter) called me and said, "Blane and Patrick (Blane's uncle and yet another Ozark Lake Mongol) have been shot!" He didn't have any other details, but he was on his way to find out. I called Ashley and had her pack an overnight bag and me and the chapter, along with St. Louis chapter, drove to the Lake in hopes our brothers were going to be okay. On the drive up, we got the call. Frank was on the scene, but no one would tell him anything. The Mongols who had remained with Blane were arrested, and police were not giving Frank any information. The first time I had met Blane was The Boogie. Because this was a three-day event, participants were given a wristband. Blane saw that as the start of his Mongol career, and refused to take off that wristband. As Frank surveyed the scene, his eyes fell on a blue tarp. Clearly there was a body underneath it. He took a deep breath and prayed it wasn't

Blane, but as he looked, he could see an arm sticking out from under the tarp, and on the arm was the wristband. Blane was dead.

*   *   *

Wichita, Kansas is right in the heart of Galloping Goose territory. We hadn't forgotten how they treated us in the Midwest, and now they were getting older and losing control of their areas. Younger Mongols were there to take their place, and we rode to Wichita to mark the setting up of a Wichita chapter. The ride home remains one of my all-time favorite club rides. Instead of interstate, we took two-lane back country highways through Kansas and into Missouri and ended up at a lake house at the Lake of the Ozarks where we stayed the night and partied at the lake. In the morning, we continued our back highway ride home. It was a few days of great weather and incredible riding, and through all of the drama that was going on, it reminded me why I loved being a Mongol. Long days on the bike, on the road, side by side with my brothers.

In early May, the Indiana Mongols had their big annual party, and a large group of us from Missouri and Illinois rode up together to support it. Since we had been working on local relationships with the Pagans, a good number of Pagans also showed up. In the past, Outlaws would come and party with us at this event, but this year it was pretty obvious that wasn't going to happen. The party went off without a hitch, and the next day we rode back toward home. Little did I know my life was about to be put on the line.

Moments earlier, we'd been enjoying the cool breeze on the open road. It had just finished raining and the air whipping past our faces smelled sweet. Behind me were almost thirty Mongols, riding wheel to wheel, handle bar to handle bar, smashing close to one hundred miles per hour in tight formation. Now, all thirty of these Mongols were crammed shoulder to shoulder inside a small Subway sandwich shop just off the interstate. Our bikes littered the parking lot, some still running. It was silent, and I could hear the slow lope of an idling Harley in the distance. And ten feet in front of me, a visibly shaken member of the Black Pistons Motorcycle Club was pointing a shiny snub-nosed revolver at my chest.

I tried to remain calm so that my men would follow suit. I didn't need anyone else drawing their weapons and turning this Subway into a shoot-out in the middle of the afternoon on what had started as a relaxing Sunday. I said, "Do you think you're the only one here with a gun?"

He shouted back, "This is our state."

I made eye contact with him. He was scared, and that wasn't good because a coward will pull the trigger instead of just taking his lumps like a man. I was trying to imagine the salesman who had sold this Piston his shiny pistol, and wondered how he convinced him he was buying the only gun in Illinois. I said, "Put that away before you get shot."

His eyes scanned the room. Many of the men had their hands in their vests, tightly gripping their pistols. Towards the far wall, a family sat in silence, staring at their sandwiches. The two employees behind the counter when we filed in had gone into the back to hide. Next to the Piston sat two Outlaws, both staring at their feet, afraid to look up.

I was starting to get mad. I said, "Why don't you put that down and you and I go outside and handle this like men?"

He wasn't even making sense now. "This state belongs to the OUTLAWS" he shouted, his voice cracked.

"Well, why don't you come outside with me and defend it?"

Silence while the man thought about his options, likely wondering if he was ready to die in a sandwich shop today. Slowly, he put the pistol back inside his cut. His confidence was gone. He looked down at the ground.

I started in on him. "Are you and I going to go outside and take care of this or not?" I was pissed and was visualizing beating the brakes off of this coward in the parking lot. The Piston didn't reply. "That's what I thought," I said, "you're just a little bitch."

"That's right," he said.

I was so stunned by his response I didn't know what to say. We all just sat there in awkward silence. I had a feeling that any moment this place would be surrounded by police, and we had already been in here far too long. I raised my right hand in the air, pointer finger up, and made a circle with it. This was the signal to mount up, we were getting out of there. Single file, we walked out of the Subway, each Mongol staring directly at the Piston and the seated Outlaws. Not one of them dared to look up from the ground. An hour before we walked into that Subway, this same group of Outlaws had been going bar to bar, telling bartenders, "We are looking for Mongols. If you see any, be sure to call and let us know." By the way they reacted when we walked in, I can assume they didn't expect to run into thirty of us. In fact, I doubt they really expected to run into any of us at all.

As we walked back to fire up our bikes, I was listening in the distance for sirens. I started to get a feeling of dread in my stomach about the potential of sitting in a jail cell instead of lying at home in my bed with my wife and dogs. I knew how upset my wife would be, how sad my mom would be. I was a social worker with a professional career to return to the next day. How would I tell them I was in jail for a gang shoot-out? I would have let a lot of people down if I ended up back in jail, fighting over territory.

As the pack roared onto the freeway, I also started to realize how close I was to getting shot. To not making it home at all. In the moment, I tried to show the guys I wasn't worried, that I didn't care, but deep inside, I was terrified. I felt like I might throw up. Over ten years ago I had gone through this, establishing the Mongols in Oregon against the wishes of the other established clubs in the region. I was a younger man then, naïve, and with something to prove. I wasn't that kid anymore. I was forty years old, a clinical therapist working with at-risk youth. I was married to the love of my life. Not only was I smarter than that naïve kid, but I knew a lot more about the biker world and how dangerous it could be. As a leader, these guys depended on me to keep them out of harm's way, yet here I was, doing the exact same thing, a decade later, in another state. About to die over a piece of cloth. Simply because it said "Illinois" and the Outlaws didn't want any other clubs in "their area." I started to get upset. I started to get angry. Apparently, these guys didn't know who I was. I had done this before, first in Oregon, then in Missouri, and now again in Illinois. I wasn't new to starting chapters in areas where we weren't welcome, and if they were going to come with a threat, they'd better back it up.

*   *   *

As I said at the beginning of this chapter, everyone wants a title until they see the work that goes with it. Whether through arrogance, naivety, or just plain ignorance, most of us would never think the decision we make could lead to the death of someone we care about. When this does happen, the leader has to take responsibility. The hardest part of leadership is owning up to something as major as having played a role in the death of a member or loved one. Blane and Tug were killed within a few months of each other, and that was arguably the hardest year of my life. I internalized the blame for Tug's death. Had I not helped him join the Pagans, perhaps he would still be with us today. Hours turn to days, to weeks, to months, and still the guilt of what ifs remains. What if I had let him join the Mongols? What if I had tried harder to intervene when I saw he had a drug problem? What if I had talked him out of joining any club and just moving on with his life? Would any of this had happened if I never moved to Illinois? The same goes for Blane. Murdered at twenty-six years old with so much of his life left to live. What if I had never let him join? What if I had taken the Goose more seriously? What could I have done differently? The fact of the matter is, in the motorcycle world, as in any world, consequences can be severe. Being in a position of leadership carries the burden of keeping your members safe and out of jail and I failed. Making choices I thought were the best ended up costing a young man his life. This is something I will live with forever. Moving to Illinois, choosing to stay active in the Mongols, choosing to start new chapters in new areas, all of those choices led to the death of two great men. I'm not sure I can ever be reconciled with that.

CHAPTER TWENTY-ONE

Letting go of my birthday party and everything we'd all enjoyed about it proved more difficult than we might have thought. We were all supposed to fly to our various homes the next day, but there was a widespread campaign to extend the fun by staying one more day. So what we decided was that, if we missed our flights, we'd stay, and, of course, we then set out to make sure we did miss them. We really dragged our asses getting to the airport. But I noticed that Blane was tapping his foot and looking anxious, so I asked him what the problem was and he explained, "Man, I can't miss this flight. I've got work; I can't miss work." He had been showing respect and hanging back with the rest of us, but he really did need to go, so I gave him and his brother permission to haul ass for the airport, and they made their flight. All the rest of us missed ours. This happened about a week before Blane was killed, and that image of him running through the airport is the last memory I have of Blane. That trip to Los Angeles was the last time we would be together.

That gave us an extra day in LA with Lil Dave. Dave and Annie were going through a rough time right then, and Dave was dealing with it by drinking heavily. I ended up spending a good part of the day doing relationship counselling, face-to-face with Dave and on the phone with Annie. Then Annie came down and joined us and we did more relationship counselling. That brought me even closer to Dave and Annie. They had already planned a trip in two weeks' time to Nashville and they invited me and Ashley to join them. We decided that was a good idea; they would fly and Ashley and I would drive down. But then everything turned to ratshit.

The day before we were due to fly to Nashville, Lil Dave called. "Hey, man, we're going to push you back a day. No big deal, I just have some personal stuff going on here."

I accepted that, didn't really give it any thought, but then, the morning we were going to fly, a text message went out from Mother chapter to everyone in the Mongol nation:

> Lil Dave is out in bad standing. He is no longer national president. He is no longer a member of the club. More information will follow.

I didn't know what to make of this. Of course, no one can be in contact with someone who is out bad and remain a Mongol. I texted Dave to ask what was going on, and he said there was nothing to worry about, he had it under control, but we'd have to cancel the trip at least for now.

I called the president of the San Diego chapter for advice on how to navigate changes in leadership when you'd been tight with the previous leadership because I knew he'd been a member for a long time, and he's been through exactly that.

Eventually, the leadership sent out a video, which had been recorded by Annie's daughter when Dave was very drunk and arguing with Annie. In this conversation, Dave said he was getting ready to leave the club. An ATF agent, John Ciccone, was in charge of monitoring the Mongols. He had been responsible for all the raids and Dave had had to work with him quite a lot to get our property back and anything connected to the ongoing RICO investigation. On the video, Dave can be heard saying: "Ciccone is retiring and we can't be protected anymore."

What he meant by those words (and bearing in mind that he was shitfaced at the time), is open to debate. Dave's version is that it had taken a long time and a huge amount of work to get Ciccone even to accept that the Mongols had a point of view, let alone try to understand what it was, and he wasn't sure, especially given the state of his marriage and the work he needed to do to save that, he had it in him to go through all that work again with a new agent. Maybe it was time to step down and let someone else take the load. That wasn't how the new Mongol leadership interpreted it; they decided it meant that Dave had been working with the ATF agent as an informant. I didn't believe that and I still don't. But a number of people had wanted to get Dave out for quite a long time, this was their opportunity, and I don't think a great deal of effort went into wondering whether Dave was telling the truth.

As I've made clear, I was a stickler for the rules from day one of my club membership. I wanted to talk to Dave, I wanted to find out how he was doing, and what was happening in his life, but the rules said no contact with anyone who had been put out bad, and so I didn't contact him.

Later, the Mongols used that video to try to get a retrial in federal court by saying that Lil Dave had been an informant and the fact had not been divulged to their lawyers. There was, though, never any proof that Dave was an informant or that he had ever given information or testified against anyone. There still isn't. If you asked my opinion now, I'd probably say that Dave was thrown out for political reasons by people who (a) didn't like him and wanted him gone, (b) wanted the power of the national presidency for themselves, and–later–(c) saw an opportunity to try to get a retrial of the case that they had previously lost. At least in the latter case, they didn't succeed.

We knew nothing of this at the time. All we knew was that Dave was out in bad standing, that serious allegations had been made about him, and that no one who wanted to continue to be a Mongol could risk contact with him.

At the outset, the new leadership told us things wouldn't change much, but of course they did. People in Mother chapter who had run against Dave or had been thrown out were brought back in. I also didn't get much support from Mother chapter when Blane was killed. The man who'd pulled the trigger was Tonka, a Galloping Goose, with whom Blane and his family had been at odds for a long time.

Due to the political changes going on at the time, Blane's death was brushed to one side. Fearing racketeering charges, Mother chapter didn't even want to acknowledge which club had killed him. The new leadership made no attempt to contact the Galloping Goose, and nor did they contact Blane's family. Like him or not, Dave would have been on the phone with both the Goose and the family the following day. I had to get the new Mongol president to call Blane's parents, and he dragged his feet on doing it.

Mike, a member of my chapter and someone who had helped me start the southern Illinois chapter, had been very close with Blane and he took his death hard. He had his issues with the Galloping Goose and with the Outlaws. One day we were out riding and, when we came back, Mike and a prospect stayed out. They went to a bar in a little town not far from Mount Vernon, and while they were there, an Outlaw and a member of an Outlaw support club showed up. Mike told them, "I'm hanging out here, and I don't want you here." They asked, in effect, "What are you going to do about it?" and Mike beat both of them up. One of them pulled out a pistol and then put it away again, but it was on someone's camera because bystanders were filming the proceedings. The Outlaw dropped his phone while he was being beaten up and a girl picked it up and, after the fight, gave it to Mike, believing it was his.

We'd received a message from Mike saying Outlaws were there, and we headed in that direction, but we couldn't contact Mike and when we arrived, we found the place surrounded by cops.

When we pieced the story together afterwards, it became clear that someone had called the cops. It was, after all, a busy bar and broad daylight. When they were asked what had happened, Mike and the Mongol prospect said they wouldn't talk without an attorney present. That is a long-standing 1 percenter rule–if you belong to a 1 percenter club, you don't give information to the police. No exceptions. But the Outlaws Mike had beaten up decided to be the exception and told the police that the Mongols had attacked them without provocation. They told law enforcement everything, even including where their gun was hidden. It was such a total breach of the 1 percenter code, I could hardly believe it had happened. You just didn't do that. Then they identified the phone that the girl had handed to Mike, and Mike was landed with a whole bunch of felony charges, including armed robbery because he had taken the phone.

They took all four back to the police station and the documentation makes clear that the Mongols had refused to provide information without an attorney being present, and that the Outlaws had provided statements and agreed to testify against the Mongols. In 1 percenter terms, that was an outrage; the code says you don't testify against another 1 percenter club member and that is simply not negotiable.

Mike spent two or three months in jail because we didn't have the money for his bail and nor did his parents. Eventually, we raised the bail money and got him out. He had to take a plea bargain because this supposed 1 percenter had agreed to testify against him at a trial, and Mike really didn't want to go to prison.

None of this did anything to improve our relationship with the Outlaws. I sent the Outlaw leadership the documentation showing just how far their member had broken the code because the normal response to having a member who had cooperated with law enforcement would be to throw him out. But that didn't happen. Grubby denied that the guy was a member of the Outlaws (in which case, why didn't he take action against him for wearing the patch?), and then changed that to say he was no longer a member; the fact is that he was and still is to this day. That's a blot on the Outlaws reputation that can never be cleared.

A couple days later, I was planning Blane's funeral, to which we took about 150 Mongols. It was a great turnout with guys riding from all over the country, and there were no issues. I was really bummed Mike couldn't be there for it. This was the second time in a short time we had flooded the lake with Mongols. Unfortunately, the second time was much more somber than the first.

When the funeral was over, I went back to LA for a president's meeting. The new leadership had a number of changes in mind, many of which would undo decisions Lil Dave had made. The one that had the biggest impact on me was that they wanted to close the Chicago chapter, and I knew I had to fight that. I hadn't been in favour of opening the Chicago chapter in the first place, I had known it would cause trouble, but we had done it, and what I didn't want to do was let down the guys who had put themselves at risk every day by wearing the patch where the Outlaws opposed it. I didn't want those guys to feel that the club was not supporting them.

I won that fight and we ended up keeping Chicago chapter.

Then in August, I flew home and Ashley and I got married. I wasn't in any doubt that this was the most important moment in my life and far outweighed anything to do with motorcycle clubs. Dave and Annie should have been there but, of course, couldn't be. The service took place at my parents' home and was wonderful–close friends and family only–and then the next day, we opened up the Oregon clubhouse and had a big party to celebrate our marriage, to which Mongols from St. Louis and the West Coast and some from the Midwest came.

Then, after another president's meeting, I went out to Miami for a big run there, not knowing that it was the last Mongol run I would ever go on.

CHAPTER TWENTY-TWO

I HAD NEVER CONSIDERED running for national president. It just wasn't something that crossed my mind. I know clubs of various kinds can suffer if most of the members are happy to enjoy the benefits of being a member, but they don't want to take on any of the hard work involved in keeping those benefits available, but that wasn't the case in any of the clubs I ever belonged to. There were always enough people who wanted the leadership positions. Sometimes, those people illustrated an idea that has been given voice many times: that the people who want positions of power are the very last who should be given them, but I never saw that as my problem. And sometimes they wanted power so badly, they were prepared to do anything, ethical or not, and moral or not, to get it. But I didn't want to be in that position. I've always felt that the people who ended up as chapter president or national president were the right people for the job, but that happened to some extent by accident because many, many people who coveted those jobs would have been very far from the right people.

For the record, I never did run for national president. But that didn't prevent people from suggesting I should, or asking me why I didn't. When I was asked questions like that, I just said I wasn't interested; it wasn't my thing. I didn't add that the motorcycle club I belonged to had ceased some time ago to be the most important thing in my life. It was true, but it took me a while to come to terms with the idea.

The Mongols were founded in California and had always been regarded as a predominantly California club. If you asked, you would be told that California had 80 percent of the membership. The rule, unwritten but understood by us all, was that if you wanted to be national president, you had to live in Los Angeles. At a president's meeting in LA to discuss elections and who would take over now that Dave was gone, that assumption was called into question. Mother chapter made it clear that no such rule existed and that anyone could run for national president. At the same time, Mother chapter was trying to get a better handle on how many Mongols there were and where they were based. The answer when it came surprised everyone: between 54 percent and 60 percent of Mongols lived outside California. Far from having 80 percent of the membership, California had less than half. It still, though, had the largest membership of any single state.

When this became well-known, people really started asking me if I intended to run for president. I still didn't, because I wasn't in the club for power, but that was exactly what the present cabinet was there for, and they began to become concerned. They didn't want to see power moving out of California away from them.

I had started the state rep program, so I had a very good relationship with the various state reps. I'd travelled a lot, I'd helped start a number of out-of-state chapters, I'd helped them with their bylaws; I had a lot of support out-of-state.

I didn't want leadership, but I did want to see greater honesty. A couple days before Miami, the leadership had started to really blacken Dave's name. Not only was he a rat, he was also a thief; he'd been helping himself to club funds. I didn't believe that then and I don't believe it now and I wasn't happy to see this campaign running.

Every club I've ever been around, when it got rid of a leader, told the membership that the leader had been stealing money. Being standard practice doesn't make it right. Most of the people making this claim had been in Dave's cabinet at the time they were now saying he'd been stealing, so what had they been doing?

I sent Mother chapter a message: "If you guys are going to say that Dave was stealing, you are either going to have to say that you didn't know what was going on, which means you're completely unfit for your position, or that you were complicit. You can't claim naivety about this; if Dave was stealing and nobody knew, then the secretary wasn't doing his job and the sarge wasn't doing his job or you guys were involved. This is a slippery slope you're setting out on."

I don't suppose sending that message did me any favors, and I don't doubt it made at least some of the cabinet want to get rid of me, but I was incensed by the way Dave's name was being trashed. I wanted them to know what it looked like to the general membership. I was tired of the mudslinging and I was trying to think about what was best for the club and not what was best for me. Getting the best for the club had always been my aim. What I hadn't realized was that members' ideas about what was best were changing. Members were joining, selection was much less stringent—really, you now just had to say you wanted to be a Mongol and you were in—and they weren't being given the introduction to the club's background they had once been given.

We were also into an age of podcasts. People were accusing Lil Dave of being a rat and he was defending himself on videos. However I feel about giving club business that sort of publicity, I understand why he did it. He'd been a Mongol for more than twenty-five years and national president for more than ten and now people who'd worked with him were badmouthing him. About two days before Miami, he had a big podcast on a big platform. Towards the end of the podcast, he suggested the club needed to make changes. His words were, "We should have a new national president, and it should be someone who is not from California, someone removed from the current politics. Someone from, like,

Oregon or Missouri." I knew when I heard it that people were going to think he was talking about me. Indeed, *I* think he was talking about me. I wasn't grateful to him because I still didn't want the job, and I knew it was going to stir up negative feelings about me in the current leadership.

When I reached Miami, the effect of that podcast was visible. Everyone was still polite and respectful, but a number of people sought me out to tell me, "You know you can't run for president unless you live in California." Up to this point, all I had been thinking about was what was best for the Mongols, but during that time in Miami, I realized there were clearly defined sides to this. What it came down to was: the current leadership against Lil Dave, and what side were you on? Two members—one who was the national president at the time and one who is now—sat me down and said, "We just want to know where your loyalties are."

I thought that was a bit rich coming from them. The guy who had taken over from Dave as national president had been Dave's best friend, so when he asked me that I said, "Listen, dude, I haven't been to Dave's house, I haven't been on his boat; you're one of his best friends. Why are you asking me about my loyalty? I was in Illinois." I was starting to get frustrated that my loyalty was questioned because I supported the leadership. I didn't support Dave; I supported the position. Dave had been put out bad and I hadn't talked to him. As time had passed, I had started to question the narrative and I didn't really agree with Dave being thrown out, but I kept that to myself because what I wanted was what was best for the club.

We had an all-members meeting in Florida and one of the first things brought up was, "You can't run for president if you don't live in California." I took that as directed at me. That was when I realized I was going to be the target of some political shit. And so it turned out. We had a meeting with all the out-of-state reps and the leadership called a vote on whether as a club we wanted to mend fences with the Outlaws or just say Fuck 'em. The overwhelming majority voted,

Fuck 'em. That was what the membership wanted, but it wasn't what the new leadership wanted, and so shortly afterwards, they started having sit-down meetings with the Outlaws to improve relations. One of the first things they did in those meetings was blame what happened on me and Dave. "We weren't aware of Chicago. Mooch shouldn't have been out there starting chapters. He had no authority to do it." This when I was the one who had argued against a Chicago chapter but gone along with it because it was a leadership decision. I was an active member, and they were throwing me under the bus. I had also told Dave I was against patching over the Bandidos, but in the end, I supported it because Dave said, "We are doing it." The leadership's position on a whole list of things that I had not wanted was, "Oh, yes, that was Mooch and Dave."

The state rep program was dismantled. Because I had a lot of support from the state reps? It was never stated, but I assume so. They gave responsibility for other states to officers living in California, which is essentially what the state rep program had been intended to change and fix–let local decisions be made by local people who understood the context.

So I left the Miami run with a bad taste in my mouth and the knowledge that I was going to be targeted. I accepted that they saw me as a threat and, if I stayed in the club much longer, I would be put out. And one of the things that followed was that I asked myself: Did I belong here any longer?

The organizations that I'd built in Oregon, in Missouri, in Illinois, and elsewhere were very structured. And the membership was changing. New members were coming in from a younger generation. Just as had always happened. And people were being patched in who would not have been patched in in earlier days. The Mongols had been built by guys who came from gangs, guys who came from the military, guys who understood rules and brotherhood, and who had already earned a name and a reputation for themselves. They'd gone through the hang around and prospect process, and they understood the Mongol ethos. Those who didn't, or who understood it but didn't feel comfortable with it, didn't make it to full membership. Now, all you needed to do was turn up and say, "I want to be a Mongol," and you'd be given the opportunity to prospect and, in some cases, handed a patch. It just wasn't the club I'd belonged to. In the past, when someone became a Mongol, they were already comfortable with themselves and putting the patch on didn't change who they were. Now, having the patch made people think that they had acquired the right to a tough guy role.

What they didn't want to do was put in the work involved in keeping a club running. They were weekend warriors, there for the parties and the image and very interested in fancy titles that suggested authority but unwilling to do the work. New members were unwilling to accept the existing structure. Why did mandatory runs have to be mandatory? Something else that caused friction was the rule that the president was the first to get on his bike and always rode up front. In fact, this was about safety–the sarge would stand next to the president, the president would get on his bike, the sarge would look around and make sure that everyone was on their bike and we wouldn't set off until that was done. I wasn't even the president, and yet people started to say, "This is an ego program. Mooch wants to get on his bike first and ride up front."

The things that I believed in were shifting and changing, and I began to realize that I probably didn't want to be part of this any longer. This was not just about the Mongols–the motorcycle club world in general was not the one I had bought into and been part of. So, I started to question what I was doing this for. I had just lost a really close brother. Tug and Blane had died. My head wasn't in a good place. Every time I put on the patch, I knew I was risking death or jail. When I believed in what we were doing and knew that everyone else believed in it, too, I didn't mind that. It was part of my life. But when I felt I wasn't supported by my own club and my brothers, it became increasingly difficult to put that patch on. Guys in California were telling me how to live my life in Illinois. The Outlaws allegedly had a contract out on my life and the leadership was telling me it was my fault when what they should have been doing was warning the Outlaws off.

I also took a good look at myself. When I joined my first club, there were always old guys who used to say, "Back in my day . . ." Now I was becoming one of the old guys and I felt like the club was looking for fewer rules and more parties and I was being selfish in wanting to stick to the old ways. If that wasn't what most members now wanted, I should probably get out of their way. The times had changed and the motorcycle club world was no longer a good fit for me. Add to that the certainty that, if I stayed, I'd be thrown out and retiring looked like the obvious choice. I talked to my own southern Illinois chapter, I talked quite a lot to Jeremy, I talked to Mother chapter, and I came to the conclusion that retiring was my best choice.

In the Mongols, if you've been in for ten years or more, you can retire in good standing. You can keep your patch, attend any club events you choose, but you will no longer be involved in club politics. So, around December 2021, that's what I did. I retired.

I decided to cover up some of my visible club tattoos. That isn't an uncommon action when people retire. For nearly fifteen years, I'd had MONGOLS tattooed on the back of my head in huge bold letters, and now here I was working in the court system, talking to probation officers and social workers and going into people's homes, and that particular tattoo didn't always help achieve the desired results. I still have tattoos that aren't visible, but I decided to cover up any visible tattoos that said Mongols. I didn't make a big deal of it, I didn't talk about it on social media, but I was posting pictures from time to time on social media and, of course, people noticed the disappearance of the tattoos. Inevitably, there were negative comments and I don't suppose it will surprise anyone who understands the human race that the people most vociferous in condemning me for covering up my Mongols tattoos were those who had sucked up to me most enthusiastically when I was in a position of leadership.

I was still following the rules, so I still hadn't contacted Lil Dave, but I did have one great resource and that was my jiujitsu team. I've seen other guys retire with nothing else to occupy their time and become very lonely, but that didn't happen to me because of the team. I'd moved to Illinois in the first place to join the jiu jitsu team, I was living (and still am) in a very small town, and, frankly, the jiujitsu team operated in some ways very like a gang. We trained together every day, members who didn't have families took their holidays together, we spent time together, and in this way, the team replaced the brotherhood I had enjoyed with motorcycle clubs but with a more positive outlook.

Mike took a plea bargain for the assault on the Outlaws and part of the plea bargain was a suspended two-year sentence during which he had regular probation sessions; one condition of his probation was that he could not associate with any known Mongol until the two years were up. Our chapter was very small but tightknit and Mike's brother, his roommate, and his coworker were all in the chapter. That meant that he couldn't see his brother, his roommate, or his coworker for two years, and that simply wasn't going to work. So the chapter was down to three or four guys, and they were forced to ask themselves whether they should (or even could) keep the chapter going. What they decided was to step away from the club at least until Mike finished his probation, and they found out what happened with me.

I'd been able to retire in good standing because I had more than ten years in. Anyone who had been a Mongol for less than ten years—and that included everyone in the chapter—and wanted to retire could only do so in bad standing unless they were given a special dispensation. What I've seen happen in other cases makes me believe that, if circumstances had been different, they would have been allowed to leave in good standing. But circumstances weren't different–the leadership saw an opportunity here to stitch me up completely. Mother chapter had been trying to change the rules so that the members could not contact not just those who were out in bad standing, but all ex-members. That was aimed entirely at me and it was just because they still feared my influence with many members. They would no longer need to push that through if they could change my status from good standing to bad standing.

I said to Mother chapter, "This town is very small, these guys are my close friends, we ride motorcycles together, we do jiujitsu together, we work out together; if you put them out bad, you put me in a very difficult position." A number of people said they would advocate for the remaining chapter members to be allowed to step back in good standing, but the fact was that they had seen the perfect opportunity to get what they wanted and, when the decision came through, it was that they were out in bad standing. When they finally telephoned to give us the result of the vote, they said, "We decided not to play favorites and to follow the rules." Then they reminded me that I was still in good standing, "but if you hang out with these guys, that will change." And they knew what the result was going to be. They asked that I not post pictures or associate with the now out bad members, and because I am a man of my word, of honor, I was upfront and told them that I would continue to be friends with the now out bad members. This was me falling on my sword. Mother chapter said they understood what I was doing, but that I was now officially out in bad standing. They sent a message out to every active member that said, "Effective immediately, Mooch is out in bad standing. There are no hard feelings towards him, he has just chosen to move on with his life." In reality, there were definitely some hard feelings.

So I was put out bad. I was asked to return my patch and all my club property and I did that. Now I was no longer allowed to associate with or talk to anyone from the club, and that was about it.

Now that I was out bad, I reached out to Lil Dave to see whether I could mend fences there.

*   *   *

My long time as a club member was over. I'd always tried to model the things we talked about. It seems to me that brotherhood, honor, and respect are just words to some people, but they are how I've tried to live my life. Standing by my chapter was the honorable thing to do. Being loyal to Lil Dave once I made sure he wasn't a rat was the brotherhood thing to do. I have to go to bed happy with my decisions and wake up happy with the man I am today. And I am, and I feel like I did the right thing.

We as a bunch of guys decided we were going to stick together. We knew what we liked out of the club world and what we didn't. We started a new movement called Lift Train Ride as a way to promote a healthier lifestyle for like-minded people. We all work out together, we do jiujitsu together, we hang out together. We get together once a week, ride together at least once a month, and once a year, we do a five-day motorcycle ride. We took all the positive parts of club life and boiled it down to the essence of what it used to be: brotherhood, riding motorcycles, and being there for each other.

I feel very fortunate. I enjoyed my time in the Mongols, I learned a lot as a Mongol, and when it was time for me to leave, I left.

CHAPTER TWENTY-THREE

A QUESTION I GET ASKED a lot is: do I miss it? And that is a tough one to answer. In all honesty, there are some things I miss, and many that I don't. There are a lot of people I miss for sure. But that is life, right? We meet people along the way, building connections that are meaningful at the time, and then drift apart as priorities and values change. Do I regret any of it? Absolutely not! The mistakes I made growing up taught me many valuable lessons and put me on the path that I am on today. They shaped who I am as a man, partner, son, and brother. My morals and values are a direct reflection of the experiences life gave me. I spent nearly a decade in the punk rock/skinhead scene and another fifteen years in the 1 percenter biker world. In those years I learned how to be a man of my word, how actions were what mattered, and how if I wanted something I had to work hard for it. Nothing was ever handed to me. And through the adversity of jail, surgery, and the loss of loved ones, I learned to value the moment, to appreciate what I have, and those I shared those moments with.

Most importantly, I am happy with the opportunity I had to make a positive influence on the worlds I moved in and the people whose lives I touched along the way. I joined the biker world in an era that was changing. When I first started coming around, the scene was still full of aging men with beards and beer bellies. Guys were dirty, on drugs, and those of us who started coming around were told if we wanted to join a club, we had to be prepared to lose our wives/girlfriends, our jobs, and possibly our freedom. As the years went on, I was able to challenge the old death or jail adage. I never understood how someone could bring a friend or loved one into a club, call them brother, and at the same time support that they lose everything. When I eventually got into leadership, I used my position to try and change that. I didn't want anyone to say that their life went downhill when they joined the Mongols. In fact, I always worked for the opposite. I wanted to see guys' lives get better when they joined the club.

Coming from a skinhead gang, the club helped me realize that my actions affected those around me. A simple bar fight could mean putting my brothers at risk of going to prison or being killed. It forced me to slow down and consider the consequences of my actions. I wanted others to do the same. I supported the brothers finding a balance between the club and their personal lives. Balance between being fathers and husbands and also good members. I wouldn't let people join who came to us when they were down because often those were the ones who left when things were good. Proving you could be a good partner and employee was a good sign you would be a good member. We encouraged, in fact it eventually became mandatory, that no one in our region was allowed to sell drugs, and everyone had to have a fulltime job or visible source of legal income. Although a lot of the members partied, no one in any of the regions I was in charge of were allowed to use meth or heroine. Brothers were allowed to party, but if we saw that it was interfering with them going to work, paying their bills, or their obligations as a club member, we would step in and offer support.

The club even had a treatment center and clean and sober chapter we could transfer members to if needed. I always suggested members workout, and when I became the regional representative for the Midwest, we voted at an all-members meeting that all active members were to workout a minimum of three days per week. I wanted brothers to do something positive for both their physical and their mental health, and also to spend time with each other outside of bars and parties. I was very strict about how members acted in public. No one was to be a bully, and members were expected to be polite to the general public. I liked challenging stereotypes and loved when I would hear when we first walked into a place we hadn't been before that people were initially scared, but when we left, they said things like, "those guys were a great group of guys, they were really nice, I wouldn't fuck with them, but I would be happy to have them on my side."

We treated the old ladies like family, sisters, and tried to make sure they were comfortable at runs and events. In Oregon, we modeled our clubhouses more on night clubs than smokey man caves. In fact, inside our clubhouses were smoke free. We wanted our parties to be a welcoming environment for women and guests. If you had a lot of women coming to your parties, the men would soon follow. And Oregon was known for some epic parties. When other clubs were still partying in dirt fields, abusing their women, and fighting each other, we were having pool parties and costume parties and having a blast. And as I said before, we made it a point to make sure whatever we did towards our prospects was meant to teach them something about the club, not for the purpose of hazing or to humiliate them.

Being in leadership offered me the opportunity to build a program that I believed was in the best interest of the nation and its members in my region. I used the club's constitution and what I learned from old-school members in Dago and Pico chapters to build bylaws that, at the time, were used by many chapters across the nation. A program built on unity and accountability. It was strict and militant, but its goal was to keep members accountable and safe ,and it gave us a look of structure that attracted like-minded men. A lot of our members came from the military or from street gangs, and structure is what kept everyone in line and on the same goal of the greater good. It was never about what was good for one person, but always what was best for the chapter and the nation. It was based on supporting the position and the structure, not the individual.

Eventually, things change, generations change, and newer members wanted fewer rules and to party more. A lot of people wanted recognition without putting in the work. And the program I had helped spread seemed to no longer be wanted. That was a hard pill to swallow. But also a good lesson, that all things must change with the times. Much as I had wanted to make our generation different than the one before me, the new crop was wanting to do the same.

My focus was always on brotherhood, riding motorcycles, and honoring tradition. That focus in my life has not changed. Since I left the club, critics have said my program was too militant, or that is was based on ego. Yet those same members were quick to take the praise and credit when that program was recognized and made them and their chapter look good. Regardless of how it is looked upon by today's generation, as long as what I helped build kept brothers out of jail, alive, and doing positive things with their lives, I believe I succeeded. I am grateful that I was able to spend close to fifteen years in a 1 percenter motorcycle club, many of those years in leadership, and not be in prison or dead. I'll take that as a win.

When asked if I have any negative feelings towards the club, that answer is simple. Absolutely not. My time in the Mongols gave me some of the best times in my life. Incredible experiences, some of the closest friends, and so many valuable lessons. It would be selfish of me to feel bad that the club moved on without me. I was never that important and am only one man. Times change. Things evolve. I am proud of the time I spent as a Mongol and take a lot of pride in the member that I was. I have no hard feelings towards the nation, and know that I made the choices that led to my being put out bad. I do not regret those decisions, and I honor the consequences. I will always look back on that time in my life fondly, without ill will, but I'm also happy to put it behind me and continue to move forward with my life. I will always have nothing but love and respect for the Mongol nation and its members; nothing will ever change that.

I sincerely hope my impact on the worlds I lived in was felt by others. I hope it inspired others. I hope, at the very least, my story inspires others to be the best version of themselves that they can be. To be the best brother they can be. The best husband they can be. The best employee, the best club member, whatever it is, that they do it with positive intention and to better themselves and those around them. That is what I consider success. It's never been about the titles, or how long you have done it, but about the impact you have had on others. I believe my impact can be felt. I am proud of the man I have become. As I age, I no longer care about the reputation as the tough guy, but I do care about a reputation as a good man. Someone that those close to me can count on, at any hour. Someone of morals and values, quick with a smile who will defend to the death those I love. I strive to continue to live with honor, for my actions to speak louder than any words, and to make those who are no longer with us, proud of what they died for. In their memory, I will live. In their memory, I will love.